Any Blonde Can Do It!

abcdefgh **A to Z** ijklmnopqrstuvwxyz

First Printing – September 2005

Copyright © 2005

ISBN Number: 0-9744972-1-5

Library of Congress Control Number: 2005908302

Printed in the United States of America
TOOF COOKBOOK DIVISION

670 South Cooper Street
Memphis, TN 38104

BLONDICATION

Any Blonde Can Do It: A to Z is a collection of recipes for all blondes, brunettes, redheads, grondes (grayheaded friends), and men (with or without hair) to show that they can do anything...even cook!

Any Blonde Can Do It: A to Z is another blonde adventure in a journey that provides fun with food. Many people have been special in the making of this cookbook. My Father, Mother, Terry, Peggy, Jim, Anne (my blonde partner), Angel, Kevin, and Bill have tolerated me. We're excited to share these recipes mixed with blonde humor and blonderful jokes. Wolfe/Sub-Zero, Minka-Aire and Kitchen Kreators have blonded my kitchen.

My brunette daughter, Chelsea, tells me repeatedly that blondes are overrated. She has been an inspiration allowing me to realize that life is a wonderful journey and that I've been blessed by the people I've traveled with each step of the way. Some gave me direction, some leant me a hand. As Chelsea reminds me, One has shown the true light that I follow, and I praise Him every day for her and all else that He has provided me with. My brunette son, Dakota has taught me patience and the true meaning of forgiveness and love.

I hope that through our cookbooks and book signings we will be able to not only give you humor and great recipes but also provide witness to the blessings we've received.

DAKOTA   CHELSEA

Tribute To
Breast Cancer Survivors

We will all be touched by breast cancer in some way. It is estimated that nearly one in eight women will be diagnosed with breast cancer in her lifetime. The other seven will know her. Some of us will lose someone we love.

There are many loving groups of breast cancer survivors. I call these groups, "sisterhood survivors" because they embrace you, lend support, answer your questions or just listen to you because they can truly relate and understand what you are going through.

To all the women who have been diagnosed with breast cancer, I say, "celebrate life to the fullest". Dare to dream big, reach down deep into your soul, and give yourself permission to not only survive but to thrive in the beauty of living life to the fullest everyday.

Be sure to love your body, not for the physical appearance but for the simple reason that it was chosen to house your soul.

My dream is about dragon boat racing for cancer survivors in the State of Louisiana. Cajun Invasion is our team's name. It is happening and I thank Debbie and Anne for being a part of the First Annual Blondes versus Bubbas Cook-Off. You girls make it so much fun and it shows not only that you are cooks with a good sense of humor, but you have hearts that are made with pure gold. We are all survivors in this world and if we join together, our souls will forever dance.

Neppie Trahan

Neppie Trahan

Breast Cancer Survivor

With Appetizers

With Appetizers

Blonde's Complaints

Us **blondes** at the offise are sew tired of awl of the dum stoopid jokes about us. We think this is hairassment. It causes us grate stress and makes our roots turn dark. We have hired a loyer and he is talking to the loyers at Blondairol. We will take this all the way to the supreme cort if we have two. Juj Thomas knos all about hairassment and he will be on are side.

We have also talked to the govner to make a new law to stop this pursicushun. We want a law that makes peepol tell brewnet jokes as much as **blonde** jokes and every so offe a read head joke.

If we don't get our way, we will not date anybody that ain't **blonde** and we will make up jokes about you and we will laff.

Sined by the **blondes** at the offise.

(Please sine with a pensil so you can erace it if you make a mistake.)

Bacon Cheese Ball
"Makin' Bacon"

1	pound bacon, fried, crumbled
2	(8 ounce) cream cheese, softened
3	Tablespoons mayonnaise
2	green onions, chopped
1	teaspoon Worcestershire
1/2	cup pecans, chopped

Combine 1st 5 ingredients together.
Refrigerate until firm.
Shape into 2 or 3 balls.
Roll in pecans.
Serve with crackers.

Dried Beef Pizza Ball
"Shrunken Italian Balls"

1	(8 ounce) sour cream
1	(8 ounce) cream cheese, softened
1	(8 ounce) cream cheese with chives/onions
1	(8 ounce) shredded pizza cheese
1	(2.25 ounce) dried beef, chopped
6	green onions, chopped

Mix all ingredients together.
Refrigerate until firm.
Shape into 2 or 3 balls.
Serve with crackers.

With Appetizers

Pepperoni Pineapple Ball
"Peppered Hospitality"

2	**(8 ounce) cream cheese, softened**
1	**(8 ounce) package pepperoni, chopped**
1	**(8 ounce) can crushed pineapple, drained**
1	**Tablespoon seasoned salt**
$^1/_2$	**bell pepper, finely chopped**
2	**Tablespoons onion, finely chopped**

Mix all ingredients together.
Refrigerate until firm.
Shape into 2 or 3 balls.
Serve with crackers.

Mexican Corn Dip
"Corny & Gay"

1	**(4 ounce) can diced jalapeños**
3	**(4 ounce) cans diced green chilies**
1	**(14 ounce) can Mexi-Corn**
1	**(8 ounce) sour cream**
$^1/_4$	**cup mayonnaise**
1	**(8 ounce) shredded cheddar cheese**
1	**(2 ounce) diced pimientos**
1	**(4 ounce) can chopped black olives**
$^1/_2$	**cup parmesan cheese**

Mix all ingredients together.
Pour into pam-sprayed 9x9 baking dish.
Bake at 350 degrees for 30 minutes.
Serve with chips.

Artichoke-Crab Dip
"Cocky & Crabby"

1¹/₂ cups parmesan cheese
1 (14 ounce) can artichokes, drained, chopped
¹/₂ cup mayonnaise
¹/₄ cup minced onions
¹/₂ teaspoon Worcestershire
¹/₄ cup breadcrumbs
¹/₈ teaspoon garlic powder
2 drops hot sauce
1 (6 ounce) can crabmeat, drained, flaked

Mix all ingredients together.
Pour into pam-sprayed 9 inch pie plate.
Bake at 350 degrees for 20 minutes.
Serve with crackers.

Wait Your Turn

After leaving a store, a **blonde** walked out and went up to a soda machine. The **blonde** put in 50 cents and out popped a coke. She searched her bag for more money. She found some and kept feeding the machine money. Coke, Sprite, and Mountain Dew bottles began rolling down the street.

A young man walked up behind her and watched this for a few minutes. Then he asked, "Can I get one now?"

She whizzed around and yelled, "No way, can't you see I'm winning?"

Spinach Dip
"Gruene With Envy"

$^1/_2$ **cup onion, finely chopped**
2   **Tablespoons olive oil**
1   **(14.5 ounce) can diced tomatoes**
1   **(4 ounce) can diced jalapeños**
1   **(10 ounce) frozen spinach, drained well**
1   **(8 ounce) cream cheese, softened**
1   **(8 ounce) shredded Monterey Jack cheese**
1   **Tablespoon red wine vinegar**
$^1/_2$ **cup milk**

Sauté onion in olive oil.
Add next 2 ingredients to onion until liquid has evaporated.
Mix next 5 ingredients in a bowl.
Combine all ingredients together.
Pour into pam-sprayed 9x13 baking dish.
Bake at 400 degrees for 25 minutes.
Serve with crackers.

Blonde's Special Order

A brunette, a redhead and a **blonde** went to an ice cream parlor together. The brunette went up and asked for a Dr. Pepper float with no ice cream. The counter man was confused, but gave her a Dr. Pepper float with no ice cream. The redhead went up and asked for a single dip of vanilla ice cream with Pepsi poured over it. The man was really confused now. But he gave the redhead her order. The **blonde** was listening to the other two women and thought that she should have a "special order" too. So she went up and asked for an extra-large root beer with no roots.

Broccoli-Cheese Squares
"Hanky Panky Bites"

$1/2$	stick margarine, melted
1	cup self-rising flour
3	eggs, beaten
1	cup milk
1	teaspoon dry mustard
2	(10 ounce) frozen chopped broccoli, drained
1	(8 ounce) shredded mozzarella cheese
1	(8 ounce) shredded cheddar cheese
$1/8$	teaspoon salt

Mix all ingredients together.
Pour into pam-sprayed 9x13 baking dish.
Bake at 350 degrees for 30 minutes.
Cut into squares when cooled.

Stuffed Cucumber Rings
"Wonder If It's Real?"

3	cucumbers
1	(8 ounce) cream cheese, softened
$1/2$	teaspoon seasoned salt
1	teaspoon lemon juice
$1^1/2$	teaspoons Worcestershire
$1/8$	teaspoon garlic salt

Peel cucumbers and remove center with apple corer.
Mix next 5 ingredients together.
Stuff cavity of cucumber with mixture.
Chill until firm.
Slice thin.

Ranch Pinwheels
"GiGi's Spinning"

- **2** (8 ounce) cream cheese, softened
- **1** package Ranch dressing mix
- **2** green onions, finely chopped
- **20** (6 inch) flour tortillas
- **1** (4 ounce) can diced green chilies
- **1** (4 ounce) can chopped black olives

Combine 1st 3 ingredients together.
Put mixture on flour tortillas.
Combine last 2 ingredients together.
Spread on tortilla and roll tightly.
Put in freezer until firm.
Slice each tortilla into 1/2 inch pieces.
Serve with salsa.

Raspberry Cheese Ring Spread
"Blondes Full Of Shan"

- **2** (8 ounce) shredded cheddar cheese
- **1** cup pecans, chopped
- **1/4** cup mayonnaise
- **1** teaspoon garlic powder
- **2** dashes hot sauce
- **1** (10 ounce) jar Blonde Raspberry Honey Jelly

Mix 1st 5 ingredients together.
Mold into a ring and chill.
Spread jelly in middle of ring.
Serve with crackers.

Artichoke Seafood Spread
"Freddie's Chokin' In Lafayette"

1/2	cup mayonnaise
1/2	cup sour cream
1	cup parmesan cheese
2	green onions, finely chopped
1	(14 ounce) can artichoke hearts, drained, chopped
1	(4.5 ounce) can tiny shrimp, drained
1/2	bell pepper, finely chopped
1	Tablespoon lemon juice
1	Tablespoon horseradish

Mix all ingredients together.
Pour into pam-sprayed 9x13 baking dish.
Bake at 400 degrees for 20-25 minutes.
Serve with crackers.

Did you hear about the Blonde who....??

Was called "Sanka" because she had no active ingredient in the bean?

Took an hour to cook Minute Rice?

Got into the taxi, and the driver kept the "Vacant" sign up?

Had a terrific stairway, but nothing upstairs?

Thought nitrates were cheaper than day rates?

With Appetizers

Spicy Salsa Spread
"Salsy & Spicy Redhead"

1   cup pecans, chopped
1   Tablespoon margarine, melted
2   (8 ounce) cream cheese, softened
1   package taco seasoning
1   (8 ounce) shredded cheddar cheese
1   cup salsa

Combine 1st 2 ingredients together.
Pour into pam-sprayed 9 inch glass pie plate.
Bake at 275 degrees for 25 minutes.
Mix next 4 ingredients together.
Pour over pecans.
Bake at 325 degrees, **covered** for 15 minutes.
Serve with chips.

God and the Blonde

A brunette, a redhead, and a **blonde** were on their way to Heaven. God told them that the stairway to Heaven was 1000 steps, and that on every 5th step He would tell them a joke. He told them not to laugh at any of the jokes along the way or else they would not be able to enter Heaven. The brunette went first and started laughing on the 45th step, so she could not enter Heaven. The redhead went next and started laughing on the 200th step, so she could not enter Heaven either. Then, it was the **blonde's** turn. When she got to the 999th step, she started laughing. "Why are you laughing?" God asked. "I didn't tell a joke." "I know," the **blonde** replied. "I just got the first joke."

At Brunch

At Brunch

Blonde Astronaut?

A **blonde**, a brunette, and a redhead were trying out for a new NASA experiment on sending women to different planets. First, they called the brunette in and asked her a question.

"If you could go to any planet, what planet would you want to go to and why?"

After pondering the question she answered, "I would like to go to Mars because it seems so interesting with all the recent news about possible extra terrestrial life on the planet."

They said "Well okay, thank you." Then told her that they would get back to her.

Next, the redhead entered the room and the NASA people asked her the same question.

In reply, "I would like to go to Saturn to see all of its rings." Again, "Thank you" and they would get back to her.

Finally, the **blonde** entered the room and they asked her the same questions they asked the brunette and the redhead. She thought for a while and replied, "I would like to go to the sun."

The people from NASA replied, "Why, don't you know that if you went to the sun you would burn to death?"

The **blonde** smirked and put her hands on her hips. "Are you guys dumb? I'd go at night!"

At Brunch

Brunch Punch
"Pat Me With A Mink"

1 (46 ounce) can pineapple juice
1 (12 ounce) can frozen orange juice, thawed
1 (12 ounce) can cream of coconut
1 teaspoon almond extract
8 cups water
1 liter ginger ale

Mix 1st 5 ingredients together and **freeze**.
Pour in punch bowl.
Add ginger ale when ready to serve.

Honey-Do Jelly Kolaches
"Jammin' Blondes"

1 (5 count) biscuits
2$\frac{1}{2}$ teaspoons Blonde Honey Jelly
2 teaspoons flour
2 teaspoons sugar
1 teaspoon margarine
Powdered sugar

Place biscuits on pam-sprayed cookie sheet.
Indent with finger in center of each biscuit.
Fill with $\frac{1}{2}$ teaspoon of honey jelly.
Mix next 3 ingredients until crumbly.
Sprinkle on top of biscuits.
Bake at 350 degrees for 15-20 minutes.
Sprinkle with powdered sugar.

17

Blueberry-Lemon Bread
"Smart, Tart & Blue"

1³/₄	cups self-rising flour
1	stick margarine, melted
1	cup sugar
2	eggs, beaten
2	teaspoons lemon juice
¹/₂	cup milk
1¹/₂	cups frozen blueberries, thawed, drained
¹/₂	cup sugar
3	Tablespoons lemon juice

Mix 1ˢᵗ 7 ingredients together.
Pour into pam-sprayed loaf pan.
Bake at 350 degrees for 1 hour.
Boil last 2 ingredients in saucepan.
Pierce bread several places with a toothpick.
Pour hot lemon mixture over loaf.

Blonde Driver's License

A **blonde** woman was speeding down the road in her little red sports car and was pulled over by a female police officer, who was also a **blonde**. The cop asked to see the **blonde's** driver's license. She dug through her purse and was getting progressively more agitated. "What does it look like?" she finally asked. The policewoman replied, "It's square and it has your picture on it." The driver finally found a square mirror, looked at it and handed it to the policewoman. "Here it is," she said. The **blonde** officer looked at the mirror, then handed it back saying, "Okay you can go, I didn't realize you were a cop."

Peach Coffee Cake
"Peachy Brain Brew"

2$^1/_3$ cups self-rising flour
1$^1/_2$ cups sugar
$^3/_4$ cup oil
$^3/_4$ cup milk
2 eggs, beaten
1 teaspoon vanilla

Combine 1st 3 ingredients until crumbly.
Set aside 1 cup of crumb mixture.
Add next 3 ingredients to remaining crumb mixture.
Pour into pam-sprayed 9x13 baking dish.
Bake at 350 degrees for 25 minutes.

Filling:
1 (3 ounce) cream cheese, softened
1 (14 ounce) can condensed milk
$^1/_3$ cup lemon juice
1 (20 ounce) can peach pie filling, mash peaches
2 teaspoons cinnamon
$^3/_4$ cup pecans, chopped

Cream all filling ingredients together.
Spoon over hot coffee cake.
Sprinkle reserved cup of crumbs over cake.
Bake another 25 minutes.

Sour Cream Coffee Cake
"Creamin' for Brew"

1	box yellow butter cake mix
1/2	cup sugar
3/4	cup oil
1	(8 ounce) sour cream
4	eggs, beaten
3	Tablespoons brown sugar

Combine 1st 6 ingredients together.
Pour into pam-sprayed 9x13 baking dish.
Bake at 350 degrees for 50-60 minutes.

Icing:

2	Tablespoons milk
1/2	teaspoon vanilla
1	cup powdered sugar

Mix all icing ingredients together.
Pour icing over cake.

Just Put It In Park

A brunette pulled into a crowded parking lot at a shopping center and rolled down the car windows to make sure her labrador retriever pup had fresh air. The lab was stretched full-out on the back seat. Impressing upon the lab to remain there, she walked to the curb backward, pointing her finger at the car and saying emphatically, "Now you stay. Do you hear me? Stay! Stay!" The driver of a nearby car, a very pretty **blonde**, gave her a strange look and said, "Why don't you just put it in park?"

Cheese Danish
"Blonde's Stuffed"

2   (8 ounce) cream cheese, softened
3/4   cup sugar
2   Tablespoons lemon juice
1   egg yolk, reserve white
1   teaspoon vanilla
2   (8 ounce) crescent rolls

Mix 1st 5 ingredients together.
Flatten a package of rolls in a pam-sprayed 9x13 baking dish.
Pour mixture over flattened rolls.
Flatten other rolls and **place** over mixture.
Brush flatten rolls with reserved egg white.
Bake at 350 degrees **uncovered** for 25-30 minutes.

Green Side Up!

A painting contractor was speaking with a redhead about her job. In the first room she said she would like a pale blue color. The contractor wrote this down and went to the window, opened it, and yelled out "GREEN SIDE UP!" In the second room she told the painter she would like it painted in a soft yellow color. He wrote this on his pad, walked to the window, opened it, and yelled "GREEN SIDE UP!" The lady was somewhat curious but she said nothing. In the third room she said she would like it painted a warm rose color. The painter wrote this down, walked to the window, opened it and yelled "GREEN SIDE UP!" The lady then asked him, "Why do you keep yelling 'green side up'?"

"I'm sorry," came the reply. "But I have a crew of **blondes** laying sod across the street.

Orange Surprise Muffins
"Orange U Glad I Did It?"

Filling:
1	(8 ounce) cream cheese, softened
1	egg, beaten
$^1/_3$	cup sugar
1	Tablespoon orange juice

Muffin:
2	sticks margarine, softened
$1^3/_4$	cups sugar
3	cups self-rising flour
1	cup milk
1	teaspoon almond extract

Beat all filling ingredients together, set aside.
Mix all muffin ingredients together.
Fill pam-sprayed muffin tins half full with muffin mixture.
Spoon 1 Tablespoon of filling mixture in each muffin tin.
Top with muffin batter.
Bake at 375 degrees for 20-25 minutes.

Blonde Sack of Potatoes

"A **blonde,** a brunette, and a redhead were being chased by the New York Police Department. They all hid from the police in a shed. The redhead hid under the hay, the brunette hid in the horse stall and the **blonde** hid in an empty potato sack. The police kicked the hay, the redhead said nothing. Then the police looked in the horse shed, the brunette said nothing nor did she move. Then the police looked at the sack of potatoes and the **blonde** said "Nothing here but a sack of potatoes."

At Brunch

Swiss Bacon Squares
"Crispy Brunette"

1	(8 count) crescent rolls
4	long slices Swiss cheese
3	eggs, beaten
1	Tablespoon onion, finely chopped
$^3/_4$	cup milk
4	slices bacon, crisp-cooked, crumbled

Press all seams of 4 crescent rolls on bottom and 1 inch up the sides of a pam-sprayed 8x8 baking dish.
Layer cheese over dough.
Whisk next 3 ingredients together.
Pour over cheese and dough.
Sprinkle crumbled bacon on mixture.
Press all seams of the remaining rolls over top of mixture.
Bake at 425 degrees for 15-20 minutes.

Ham-Vegetable Scramble
"Scrambling to Meet"

12	eggs, beaten
1	cup ham, chopped
1	bell pepper, chopped
1	small onion, chopped
1	large tomato, chopped
1	(8 ounce) shredded cheddar cheese

Mix all ingredients together.
Pour into pam-sprayed 9x13 baking dish.
Bake at 325 degrees for 1 hour.

At Brunch

Sausage-Cheese Bake
"Wake Me Up Before You Go-Go"

1 (8 count) crescent rolls
1 pound hot pork sausage, cooked, drained
5 eggs, beaten
3/4 cup milk
1/2 teaspoon each salt & pepper
1 (8 ounce) shredded mozzarella cheese

Place crescent rolls in pam-sprayed 9x13 baking dish.
Press seams together and **cover** with sausage.
Combine remaining ingredients in separate bowl.
Pour over sausage.
Bake at 350 degrees for 30 minutes.

Sausage-Hashbrown Casserole
"A Blonde Whiz"

1 pound sausage, browned, drained
1 (32 ounce) bag frozen hash brown potatoes
1 can cream of chicken soup
1 (8 ounce) jar Cheez Whiz
1 (8 ounce) sour cream
Salt & pepper to taste

Mix all ingredients together.
Pour into pam-sprayed 9x13 baking dish.
Bake at 350 degrees for 1 hour.

Q: Why did the blonde golfer wear two pairs of shoes?
A: In case she got a hole in one.

Sausage Links
"Link Me to Your Bed"

8	slices bread, cubed
1$^1/_2$	pounds link sausage, browned, cut into thirds
1	(16 ounce) shredded cheddar cheese
4	eggs, beaten
2$^1/_4$	cups milk
$^3/_4$	teaspoon dry mustard
	Salt & pepper to taste
1	can cream of mushroom soup
$^1/_2$	cup milk

Layer 1st 3 ingredients in pam-sprayed 9x13 baking dish.
Combine next 3 ingredients together.
Pour over bread layers.
Refrigerate overnight.
Combine last 3 ingredients together.
Pour over mixture.
Bake at 300 degrees for 1 hour and 15 minutes.

Blonde, Brunette & Redhead with a Genie

A **blonde** a brunette and a redhead were all on a deserted island. A genie appeared and said each of them gets a wish. The redhead wished she was home eating supper with her family. The brunette wished she was home eating supper with her family also. The **blonde** said to the genie, "I'm lonely I wish my friends were here."

At Brunch

Who Says We Are Stupid?

80,000 **blondes** are in a huge stadium for a 'Blondes Are Not Stupid Convention.' The announcer says "We are all here today to prove to the world that **blondes** are not stupid. Can I have a volunteer?" One **blonde** steps up. The announcer says to her, "What's 15 plus 15?" After 15 or 20 seconds she says, "Eighteen." Obviously everyone is a little disappointed. 79,999 **blondes** start cheering, "Give her another chance, give her another chance." The announcer says, "Well, since we've gone to the trouble of getting 80,000 of you and the world-wide press here, I guess we can give her another." So he says, "What is 5 plus 5?" After nearly 30 seconds she eventually says, "Ninety?" the announcer sighs – everyone is crestfallen the **blonde** starts crying and 79,999 **blondes** start cheering, "Give her another chance, give her another chance." The announcer, unsure whether or not he is doing more harm than good, eventually says, "OK, last chance, what's 2 plus 2?" the girl dries her eyes and after a whole minute eventually says, "4." Around the stadium 79,999 girls start yelling "Give her another chance, give her another chance."

At Christmas

At Christmas

She Was So Blonde That She...

1. Took her new scarf back to the store because it was too tight.
2. Couldn't learn to water ski because she couldn't find a lake with a slope.
3. Couldn't work in a pharmacy because the bottles won't fit into the typewriter.
4. Got excited because she finished a jigsaw puzzle in 6 months and the box said 2 to 4 years.
5. Was trapped on an escalator for hours when the power went out.
6. Couldn't call 911 because there was no 11 on any phone button.
7. When asked what the capital of California was, she answered C.
8. Burnt her nose bobbing for French fries.
9. Baked a turkey for 5 days because the instructions said 1 hour per pound and she weighed 125 pounds.
10. Couldn't make Kool-Aid because 8 cups of water wouldn't fit into those little packets.
11. Changes the baby's diaper only once a month because the label said good up to 20 pounds.

At Christmas

Holiday Punch
"Rudolph's Nosey"

1	**(6 ounce) can frozen orange juice, thawed**
2	**cups water**
1	**(46 ounce) can red tropical punch**
$1/2$	**(46 ounce) can pineapple juice**
$1/2$	**(48 ounce) bottle cranapple juice**
1	**2 liter ginger ale, chilled**

Combine 1st 5 ingredients together.
Chill and **pour** in punch bowl.
Add ginger ale before serving.

Cranberry-Pumpkin Muffins
"Santa's Pilgrims Muffs"

2	**cups self-rising flour**
$1/2$	**teaspoon cinnamon**
$1/2$	**teaspoon allspice**
$1/2$	**teaspoon nutmeg**
$1/3$	**cup oil**
2	**eggs, beaten**
1	**(15 ounce) can pumpkin**
$1/2$	**cup milk**
1	**(16 ounce) can whole cranberry sauce**

Mix all ingredients together.
Pour into pam-sprayed muffin tins.
Bake at 300 degrees for 20-30 minutes.

At Christmas

Christmas Morning Breakfast
"A Cold Breeze"

3	cups croutons
3	cups ham, cooked, chopped
1	(16 ounce) shredded cheddar cheese
6	eggs, beaten
3	cups milk
1	teaspoon prepared mustard
1/2	cup onion, finely chopped
1	(8 ounce) can sliced mushrooms
	Salt & pepper to taste

Layer in order 1st 3 ingredients in pam-sprayed 9x13 dish.
Mix next 6 ingredients together.
Pour over layers, chill overnight.
Bake at 325 degrees for 45 minutes.

Cranberry-Sour Cream Salad
"Frosty Is Berry Creamy"

1	small cherry gelatin
1	cup hot water
1	cup cold water
1	(16 ounce) can whole cranberry sauce
3	celery ribs, finely chopped
1	(8 ounce) sour cream

Dissolve gelatin in hot water.
Add cold water to gelatin until thickened.
Combine last 3 ingredients with gelatin.
Pour into 9x13 dish.
Chill until firm.

Cranberry Pudding Cake
"Berry Good Shaky Puddin'"

1 box yellow cake mix
1 small lemon instant pudding
4 eggs, beaten
1 (8 ounce) sour cream
1/4 cup oil
1 (16 ounce) can jellied cranberry sauce, cut into small cubes

Combine 1st 5 ingredients together.
Fold in cranberry cubes.
Pour into pam-sprayed 9x13 baking dish.
Bake at 350 degrees for 50-55 minutes.

Raspberry-Blueberry Salad
"Pink And Blue Poinsettia"

1 large raspberry gelatin
1 cup boiling water
1 (20 ounce) can blueberry pie filling
1 (8 ounce) can crushed pineapple
1 cup chopped pecans
1 (8 ounce) carton whipped topping

Mix 1st 2 ingredients together.
Add next 3 ingredients to gelatin.
Refrigerate for 30 minutes.
Fold in whipped topping.
Pour into pam-sprayed 9x13 dish. **Chill**.

Turkey-Cranberry Salad
"Layering Her Garland"

Layer 1:
- 1   (3 ounce) envelope unflavored gelatin
- 1/4 cup cold water
- 1   (16 ounce) can whole cranberry sauce
- 1   (8 ounce) can crushed pineapple with juice
- 1/4 cup sugar
- 1   cup pecans, chopped

Layer 1:
Combine 1st 2 ingredients, set aside.
Combine next 3 ingredients in saucepan, heat to boiling point.
Add gelatin mixture, stir well.
Mix in pecans.
Pour into pam-sprayed 9x13 glass dish. **Chill**.

Layer 2:
- 1   (3 ounce) envelope unflavored gelatin
- 1/4 cup cold water
- 1/2 cup water
- 1   (3 ounce) cream cheese, softened
- 3   Tablespoons lemon juice
- 2   cups turkey, cooked, chopped

Layer 2:
Combine 1st 5 ingredients in saucepan.
Bring to a boil, **stir** until cream cheese dissolves.
Fold in turkey.
Pour layer 2 onto layer 1. **Chill.**

Sweet Potato Casserole
"Hammering Studs With Stomps"

3	**sweet potatoes, boiled, mashed**
$^1/_3$	**cup evaporated milk**
$^3/_4$	**cup sugar**
2	**eggs, beaten**
$^1/_2$	**stick margarine, melted**
1	**teaspoon vanilla**

Mix all ingredients together.
Pour into pam-sprayed 9x13 baking dish.

Topping:

1	**cup brown sugar**
$^1/_3$	**cup margarine, melted**
$^1/_2$	**cup flour**
1	**teaspoon vanilla extract**
1	**teaspoon almond extract**
1	**cup pecans, chopped**

Mix all ingredients together.
Sprinkle on top of sweet potato mixture.
Bake at 350 degrees for 30-40 minutes.

Crunchy Vegetable Bake
"The Grinch that Crunched Christmas"

1	can cream of celery soup
1	(8 ounce) sour cream
3	celery ribs, chopped
$1/2$	green bell pepper, chopped
$1/2$	red bell pepper, chopped
1	(8 ounce) shredded cheddar cheese
1	(16 ounce) can shoe peg corn, drained
1	(16 ounce) can green beans, drained
2	cups Waverly crackers, crushed

Mix 1st 8 ingredients together.
Pour into pam-sprayed 9x13 baking dish.
Sprinkle with crackers.
Bake at 350 degrees for 30-40 minutes.

Ham-Potato Stick Combo
"Elves Sticking Around"

1	carrot, grated
2	ribs of celery, finely chopped
$1/2$	onion, finely chopped
$1/3$	cup mayonnaise
1	teaspoon jalapeño mustard
$1/3$	cup sweet pickle relish
$1/2$	teaspoon salt & pepper
2	cups ham, cooked, chopped
1	(1.5 ounce) can shoestring potato sticks

Combine all ingredients together. **Serve** at room temperature.

Cranberry Pork Loin
"Ring My Bell"

1	(2-3 pound) boneless pork loin
1	(16 ounce) can jellied cranberry sauce
$1/2$	cup cranberry juice
$1/2$	cup sugar
1	teaspoon dry mustard
$1/4$	teaspoon ground cloves
2	Tablespoons cornstarch
2	Tablespoons cold water
$1/2$	teaspoon salt

Place 1st 6 ingredients in crock pot for 6-8 hours on low.
Remove roast and **place** on platter.
Pour juices from crock pot into sauce pan.
Mix cornstarch in cold water, **mixing** well.
Add to juices on stove.
Cook and **stir** until thickened.
Add salt.
Pour sauce over pork.

Q: There was a Smart Blonde, a Dumb Blonde, Santa Claus, and the Easter Bunny sitting around a table with $10,000 in the middle of it. Who do you think will get the money?
A: The Dumb **blonde** because there is no such thing as a Smart **blonde**, Santa Claus, or the Easter Bunny.

Turkey & Dressing Bake
"Dressing Up for Santa"

1 (8 ounce) package stuffing
3 cups turkey, cooked, diced
1 (4 ounce) can chopped green chilies
1 red bell pepper, chopped
1 can cream of chicken soup
1 (8 ounce) sour cream
$^1/_2$ cup water
$^1/_2$ stick margarine, melted
1 (8 ounce) shredded mozzarella cheese

Mix 1st 8 ingredients together.
Pour into pam-sprayed 2 quart baking dish.
Bake at 350 degrees covered for 30-40 minutes.
Uncover, sprinkle with cheese.
Bake for 5 more minutes.

Blonde Christmas Tree

There were two **blondes** who went deep into the frozen woods searching for a Christmas tree. After hours of subzero temperatures and a few close calls with hungry wolves, one **blonde** turned to the other and said... "I'm chopping down the next tree I see. I don't care whether it's decorated or not!"

At Deer Camp

At Deer Camp

Blonde Hunter

Two brunette men and a **blonde** man go hunting. They arrive at the hunting cabin, and get all set up. The next day, the first brunette hunter goes out. He returns with a big deer. The second two guys ask him how he did that. They can't believe how big the deer is.

"It was easy. Found the tracks, followed the tracks, BAM! Shot the deer."

The next day, the second brunette hunter goes out, and comes back with an even bigger deer. The **blonde** guy's eyes bug out when he sees it, and he asks him how he did it.

"Same thing the first guy did. Found the tracks, followed the tracks, BAM! Shot the deer."

So on the third day, the **blonde** guy goes out to hunt. He doesn't come back for a very long time. When he staggers into the cabin, rifle gone, all beat up and bruised, with only one boot, the other two were very surprised.

They asked him what happened.

"Well, I found the tracks, followed the tracks and BAM! Got hit by a train."

Jalapeño Stuffed Dove
"Flying Hot & Stuffed"

12   **doves, cleaned**
1   **(16 ounce) bottle Italian dressing**
12   **jalapeño sliced peppers**
1   **pound of bacon, cut in half**
     Blonde's All-Purpose Seasoning
     Blonde's Lemon-Pepper

Marinate doves in dressing for at least 2 hours.
Cut dove breast away from the bone.
Place a sliced pepper in each breast.
Wrap bacon around each breast.
Secure with toothpick.
Season well with seasonings.
Cook on grill, turning several times.

Tracks Galore!

Three **blondes** were walking through a forest when they came upon a set of tracks.

The first **blonde** looked down at the tracks and said, "I think these are bird tracks."

The second **blonde** looked at them and said, "No, these are deer tracks."

The third **blonde** looked down, and BOOM!!! she gets run over by a train.

Wine-Dove
"White-Winged Drunk"

- **1** cup flour
- **1** teaspoon salt
- **1** teaspoon pepper
- **12** doves
- **1/2** cup oil
- **1/2** cup water
- **1** can cream of mushroom soup
- **1** rib of celery, chopped
- **1/2** cup red wine

Mix 1st 3 ingredients together.
Toss doves in seasoned flour.
Brown doves in oil.
Pour off excess oil.
Place doves in 2 quart baking dish.
Combine last 4 ingredients.
Pour over doves.
Bake at 350 degrees covered for 2 1/2 hours.

Q: Why didn't the blonde go to the movies on buck night?
A: Because she couldn't fit the deer into the car.

At Deer Camp

Duck Casserole
"She's All Quacked Up"

2¹/₂	cups cooked duck, chopped
1	(8 ounce) shredded cheddar cheese
¹/₂	teaspoon Blonde Lemon-Pepper
3	(14 ounce) cans chicken broth
1	onion, chopped
5	ribs of celery, chopped
¹/₂	teaspoon salt
1	can cream of mushroom soup
4	sleeves Ritz crackers, crushed, reserve 1 cup

Combine all ingredients. **Mix** well.
Pour into pam-sprayed 9x13 baking dish.
Sprinkle with remaining crumbs.
Bake at 350 degrees for 45 minutes.

One Brick Shy

A brunette, a **blonde**, and a redhead were standing in a line before a firing squad. The commander says, "READY, AIM" and the brunette yells "TORNADO!" All the people turned around and looked and the brunette ran away.

Next, it's the redhead's turn. The commander says, "READY, AIM" and the redhead yells "HURRICANE!" Once again all the people turned around to look for the hurricane and the redhead runs away.

Finally, it's the **blonde's** turn. The commander says, "READY, AIM" and the **blonde** yells "FIRE!"

Smoked Duck Breast
"Quacked Up Breasts"

6	duck breasts, cleaned
1	(16 ounce) bottle Italian dressing
$1/2$	teaspoon salt
$1/2$	teaspoon garlic salt
$1/2$	teaspoon pepper
$1/2$	teaspoon Blonde Lemon-Pepper
6	strips of bacon
1	stick margarine, melted
3	Tablespoons Worcestershire

Marinate duck breast in Italian dressing 4-8 hours.
Remove breasts from marinade.
Sprinkle with both salts and peppers.
Wrap bacon around breasts and **secure** with toothpick.
Mix last 2 ingredients and **baste** over duck.
Cook on grill, **basting** and **turning** several times.

CAUTION: Blonde Men Working

There were two **blonde** guys working for the city. One would dig a hole, the other would follow behind him and fill the hole in. They worked furiously all day without rest, one guy digging a hole, the other guy filling it in again. An onlooker was amazed at their hard work, but couldn't understand what they were doing. So he asked the hole digger, "I appreciate the effort you are putting into your work, but what's the story? You dig a hole and your partner follows behind and fills it up again." The hole digger wiped his brow and sighed, "Well, normally we are a three-man team, but the guy who plants the trees is sick today."

At Deer Camp

Venison Chili
"Pink House AdVANCED"

2	pounds ground venison, browned, drained
1	onion, chopped
1/2	teaspoon garlic salt
3	teaspoons salt
4	Tablespoons chili powder
1	Tablespoon cumin
1	can tomato soup
1	(15 ounce) can kidney beans
2	cups water

Combine all ingredients together.
Simmer for 1 hour.

Pepper Tomato Venison Soup
"Pep Me Up Dear"

1¹/₂	pounds ground venison, browned, drained
3	bell peppers, chopped
1	onion, chopped
2	(10.5 ounce) cans beef broth
2	cans tomato soup
1	(15 ounce) can stewed tomatoes
1¹/₂	cups rice, cooked

Combine 1st 6 ingredients together in large saucepan.
Bring to a boil. **Simmer** for 30 minutes.
Add rice. **Return** to simmer.

Venison Marinade
"Dear, I'm All Soaked Up"

³/₄	**cup red wine**
¹/₂	**cup soy sauce**
¹/₂	**cup Italian dressing**
1	**teaspoon onion salt**
1	**teaspoon pepper**
1	**teaspoon garlic salt**

Soak deer meat in milk 2-4 hours.
Remove and **place** in dish.
Cover with marinade.
Marinade overnight.

Who! Who!

Ashley, a **blonde**, was seen going into the woods with a small package and a large bird cage. She was gone several days, but finally she returned.

Her friend, Chelsea, never saw Ashley looking so sad. "Heard you went off into the woods for a couple of days. Glad you got back okay. But you look so sad. Why?"

Ashley said, "Cause I just can't get a man."

Chelsea replied, "Well, you sure won't find one in the middle of the woods."

Ashley said, "Don't be so silly. I know that. But I went into the woods because I needed to find something there that would get me a man. But I couldn't find it."

Chelsea said, "I don't understand what you're talking about."

Ashley replied, "Well, I went there to catch a couple of owls. I took some dead mice and a bird cage."

Chelsea asked, "So, how is that gonna help you get a man."

Ashley answered, "Well, I heard the best way to get a man is to have a good pair of hooters."

At Deer Camp

Venison Meatloaf
"Dear Loafin' for Meat"

1	pound ground venison
1	egg, beaten
4	saltine crackers, crushed
1/4	cup milk
1/2	onion, chopped
1	(8 ounce) can tomato sauce
1	Tablespoon Worcestershire
1	Tablespoon brown sugar
	Salt & pepper to taste

Mix 1st 5 ingredients together, thoroughly.
Put mixture in loaf pan.
Combine last 4 ingredients.
Pour over meat loaf.
Bake at 350 degrees for 1 hour.

Venison Round Steak
"Stakin' A Dear"

1/4	cup flour
2	teaspoons dry mustard
2	teaspoons salt & pepper
2	teaspoons Worcestershire
1	pound venison steak, tenderized
1/4	cup oil

Combine 1st 4 ingredients together.
Dip venison into flour mixture.
Pan-fry venison in oil until done.

45

Venison Meatballs
"Foozie Hunting Dear"

1	**pound ground venison**
¹/₂	**cup bread crumbs**
1	**egg, beaten**
1	**teaspoon salt**
¹/₄	**teaspoon pepper**
¹/₄	**teaspoon garlic powder**
¹/₄	**teaspoon Blonde All-Purpose Seasoning**
1	**Tablespoon oil**
¹/₂	**cup water**

Mix 1ˢᵗ 7 ingredients together, thoroughly.
Shape into walnut size balls.
Brown in hot oil. **Drain**.
Add ¹/₂ cup water and **simmer** meatballs for 30 minutes.
Add to favorite sauce.

A Hunting We Will Go

One day two **blondes** go duck hunting. Neither of them had been duck hunting before and after several hours they had shot nothing. The one **blonde** looked at the other and said, "I just don't understand it. Why haven't we caught anything yet?" Her friend answered, "Maybe we're not throwing the dog high enough."

Venison Sausage & Rice
"Dear, Weiner & Muff"

1   onion, chopped
1   bell pepper, chopped
1   Tablespoon oil
1   pound ground deer sausage
     Salt & pepper to taste
1   can cream of mushroom soup
1   can cream of chicken soup
1¹/₂   cans water
1   cup rice, cooked

Sauté onion and bell pepper in oil.
Add next 5 ingredients to mixture.
Bake at 350 degrees for 1 hour.
Serve over rice.

Tennis Elbow

One day while jogging, a middle-aged man noticed a tennis ball laying by the side of the walk. Being fairly new and in good condition, he picked the ball up, put it in his pocket and proceeded on his way.

Waiting at the cross street for the light to change, he noticed a beautiful young **blonde** woman standing next to him smiling.

"What do you have in your pocket? she asked. "Tennis ball," the man said smiling back.

"Wow," said the **blonde** looking very upset. "That must hurt. I once had tennis elbow and the pain was unbearable!"

Venison Roast
"A Roasted Toasted Dear"

1	**(3 to 4 pounds) venison roast**
¹/₄	**cup balsamic vinegar**
¹/₄	**cup minced garlic**
¹/₂	**cup onion, chopped**
1	**(8 ounce) can tomato sauce**
1	**Tablespoon ground mustard**
1	**package brown gravy mix**
2	**Tablespoons salt**
¹/₄	**cup water**

Combine all ingredients in crock-pot.
Cook on high for 5 hours.

A Blonde Man's Wish

Three **blonde** men were walking through the desert when they found a magic genie's lamp. The genie said, "I will grant three wishes, one for each of you."

The first **blonde** guy said, "I wish I were smarter." So he became a redhead.

The second **blonde** man said, "I wish I were smarter than he is." The genie granted his wish and he became a brunette.

The third **blonde** man said, "I wish I were smarter than both of them." The genie said, "Okay." So he became a **blonde** woman.

At Easter

At Easter

Three Blondes and St. Peter

Three **blondes** died and found themselves standing before St. Peter. He told them that before they could enter the Kingdom, they had to tell him what Easter was. The first **blonde** said, "Easter is a holiday where they have a big feast and we give thanks and eat turkey." St. Peter said, "Noooooo," and he banished her. The second **blonde** said, "Easter is when we celebrate Jesus' birth and exchange gifts." St. Peter said, "Noooooo," and he banished her also. The third **blonde** said she knew what Easter was, and St. Peter said, "So, tell me." She said, "Easter is a Christian holiday that coincides with the Jewish festival of Passover. Jesus was having Passover feast with His disciples, when he was betrayed by Judas, and the Romans arrested him. The Romans hung Him on the cross and eventually He died. Then they buried Him in a tomb behind a very large boulder." St. Peter said, "Verrrrrry good." Then the **blonde** continued, "Now every year the Jews roll away the boulder and Jesus comes out. If he sees his shadow, we have six more weeks of winter."

At Easter

Deviled-Egg Spread
"Deviled Jim Hunt"

3	hard-boiled eggs, mashed
1	(3 ounce) cream cheese, softened
1	(8 ounce) shredded Monterrey Jack cheese
$1/2$	cup mayonnaise
$1/2$	teaspoon prepared mustard
$1/2$	teaspoon salt
$1/2$	teaspoon pepper
$3/4$	cup pecans, chopped
1	(4 ounce) can chopped green chilies

Mix all ingredients together.
Serve with crackers.

Stuffed Deviled-Eggs
"Miniature Angel Egg"

6	eggs, hard boiled, peeled
2	teaspoons prepared mustard
$1^1/2$	teaspoons Worcestershire
2	teaspoons lemon juice
$1/4$	cup sour cream
	Salt & pepper to taste

Cut eggs in half lengthwise.
Remove yolk and **mash**.
Combine next 5 ingredients with yolk.
Place in eggs whites.

Butter Mint Salad
"Mint to be Buttered Up"

2 (16 ounce) cans crushed pineapple, drained
1 large box lime gelatin
1 (12 ounce) frozen whipped topping
1 teaspoon pineapple extract
1/2 teaspoon mint extract
1 (8 ounce) box butter mints, crushed

Mix 1st 2 ingredients, set overnight at room temperature
Fold in next 4 ingredients.
Pour into 9x9 glass dish and freeze.

Cashew Salad
"Nut Case Blonde"

1 large box lemon gelatin
1 cup boiling water
1 quart vanilla ice cream
1 (15 ounce) can fruit cocktail, drained
1 (11 ounce) can mandarin oranges, drained, chopped
1 1/4 cups cashews, chopped

Dissolve gelatin in boiling water.
Mix all ingredients together.
Pour into 9x13 glass dish.
Refrigerate overnight.

Easter Fruit Salad
"Fruity Rabbit Tricks Are For Kids"

1   **(20 ounce) can pineapple chunks, drained**
1   **(16 ounce) can peach halves, drained**
1   **(16 ounce) can pear halves, drained**
1   **(11 ounce) can mandarin oranges, drained**
2   **bananas, sliced**
$1/2$ **cup brown sugar**

Layer 1st 5 ingredients in 9x13 baking dish in order given.
Sprinkle brown sugar over fruit.
Bake at 350 degrees for 30 minutes.

Pear-Lime Salad
"Bradford Party Tarty"

1   **small box lime gelatin**
1   **cup boiling water**
1   **(16 ounce) can pear halves, diced, reserving**
     $3/4$ cup syrup
1   **Tablespoon lemon juice**
1   **(8 ounce) cream cheese, softened**
$1/8$ **teaspoon cinnamon**

Dissolve gelatin in boiling water.
Add reserved syrup & lemon juice.
Pour into loaf pan. **Chill** until set, about 1 hour.
Mix last 2 ingredients together with diced pears.
Fold all ingredients into loaf pan. **Chill**.

Easter Lamb Soup
"A Sheep In Wool Clothing"

2	Tablespoons olive oil
1	onion, finely chopped
4	(14 ounce) cans chicken broth
1	(2 pound) lamb roast, cut in $^1/_4$ inch pieces
$^1/_2$	cup Italian seasoning
$^1/_2$	cup fresh dill
$^1/_3$	cup long-grain rice
4	large egg yolks, beaten
$^1/_2$	cup lemon juice

Sauté 1st 2 ingredients in a large stockpot about 5 minutes.
Add next 4 ingredients. **Bring** to a boil.
Cover. **Simmer** for 1 hour.
Add rice. **Simmer** about 20 minutes.
Beat last 2 ingredients until frothy.
Combine all ingredients. **Stir**.
Simmer for 1 minute. Do NOT boil.

Died And Gone To Heaven

A **blonde** died and went to Heaven. When she got to the Pearly Gates, she met St. Peter who said, "Before you get to come into Heaven, you have to pass a test." "OH, NO!" exclaimed the **blonde**.

But St. Peter said not to worry, because he would make it an easy test. "Who was God's son?" asked St. Peter.

The **blonde** thought for a few minutes and replied,"Andy." "Andy? That's interesting. What made you say that?" inquired St. Peter.

Then the **blonde** started to sing, "Andy walks with me. Andy talks with me. Andy tells me…"

Blonde Potato Salad
"Deb's Studded Chunk"

6	potatoes, peeled, boiled, cut in wedges
1/2	cup oil
1/4	cup Creole mustard
2	Tablespoons Dijon mustard
2	Tablespoons Worcestershire
1/2	teaspoon cayenne pepper
1	onion, finely chopped
2	ribs of celery, finely chopped
	Salt & pepper to taste

Combine all ingredients together.
Gently toss. **Refrigerate.**

Orange-Pecan Ham
"Orange You Glad She's A Nutty Porker?"

1	(4 pound) ham
1	(6 ounce) can frozen orange juice, thawed
1	cup pecans, chopped
1/2	cup brown sugar
1/4	teaspoon ground cloves
1/4	teaspoon nutmeg

Place ham in 9x13 baking dish.
Bake at 325 degrees **covered** for 1 hour.
Combine rest of ingredients together.
Pour glaze over ham. **Bake** for 40 more minutes.

At Easter

Honey Mustard Tenderloin
"Honey My Loin"

1	**(16 ounce) bag peeled baby carrots**
12	**new potatoes**
6	**cups water**
$^1/_3$	**cup honey mustard**
2	**Tablespoons olive oil**
1	**(3-5 pound) pork tenderloin**

Cook 1st 3 ingredients in large saucepan until boiling. **Drain**.
Combine next 2 ingredients together.
Toss carrots and potatoes with mustard mixture. **Add** 2 cups of water.
Place in pan around tenderloin in 9x13 baking dish.
Bake at 425 degrees **covered** for 25-35 minutes.
Stir vegetables once.
Bake uncovered for 30-40 more minutes.

Safety First!

A **blonde's** car breaks down on the interstate one day. So she eases it over onto the shoulder of the road. She carefully steps out of the car and opens the trunk.

Out of the trunk jump two men in trench coats who walk to the rear of the vehicle where they stand facing oncoming traffic and begin opening their coats and exposing their nude bodies to approaching drivers.

Not surprisingly, one of the worst pile-ups in history of this highway occurs. It's not very long before a police car shows up. The cop, clearly enraged, runs toward the **blonde** of the disabled vehicle yelling, "What the heck is going on here?"

My car broke down, says the lady, calmly.

"Well, what are these guys doing here by the road?" asks the cop. And she replies, "Hellooo! Those are my emergency flashers!"

56

Mandarin Orange Cake
"Orange You Demanding A Ring?"

1	box butter cake mix
³/4	cup oil
4	eggs, beaten
1	(11 ounce) can mandarin oranges, with juice
1	small box instant vanilla pudding
1	(12 ounce) frozen whipped topping

Mix 1st 3 ingredients together.
Pour into 2 pam-sprayed round cake pans.
Bake at 350 degrees for 20-30 minutes.
Mix last 3 ingredients.
Spread between cake layers, on top & sides.
Refrigerate.

Vanilla Chip Cake
"A Chipper Bleached Blonde"

1	box white cake mix
1	(3 ounce) box instant vanilla pudding
1	(16 ounce) sour cream
5	eggs, beaten
1	stick margarine, melted
1	(12 ounce) white chocolate chips

Mix 1st 5 ingredients thoroughly.
Fold in chips.
Pour into pam-sprayed bundt pan.
Bake at 350 degrees for 50-60 minutes.

At Easter

Magic

Once there was this guy, and he was driving in his car, and all of a sudden, he sees the Easter Bunny hopping on the road. He was going too fast, and he didn't hit the brakes in time, so he hit the Easter Bunny.

He was really upset, and was thinking, "Oh no, what about all those poor little kids?? What can I do!?" Then, a **blonde** drove up in her car, and asked, "What's wrong?"

"I hit the Easter Bunny!!" said the guy.

"Oh, I know what to do," said the **blonde**, and she went into her car, got a can, and sprayed the Easter Bunny with it.

A few minutes later, the Easter Bunny got up, hopped a little bit, turned around and waved, hopped a little, turned around and waved, and it kept doing that.

When the Easter Bunny was out of sight, the guy turned to the **blonde** and asked, "Wow, I'm dying to know what was in that can!"

"Oh," said the **blonde**, "It was hair spray. It says, 'Spray on dead hair for permanent wave.'

With Fruit

With Fruit

Blonde Bird Question

A **blonde** named Lisa is appearing on "Who Wants To Be A Millionaire?" with Regis Philbin. Regis: "Lisa, you're up to $500,000 with one lifeline left: phone a friend. If you get it right, the next question is worth one million dollars. If you get it wrong, you drop back to $32,000. Are you ready?" Lisa: "Yes." Regis: "Which of the following birds does not build its own nest? Is it A) robin, B) sparrow, C) cuckoo, or D) thrush." Lisa: "I'd like to phone a friend. I'd like to call Debbie." Debbie (also a **blonde**) answers the phone: "Hello?" Regis: "Hello Debbie, it's Regis Philbin from Who Wants to be a Millionaire. I have your friend Lisa here who needs your help to answer the one million dollar question. The next voice you hear will be Lisa's..." Lisa: "Debbie, which of the following birds does not build its own nest? Is it A) robin, B) sparrow, C) cuckoo, or D) thrush?" Debbie: "Oh geez, Lisa. That's simple. It's a cuckoo." Lisa: "Are you sure?" Debbie: "I'm sure." Regis: "Lisa, you heard Debbie. Do you keep the $500,000 or play for the million?" Lisa: "I want to play; I'll go with C) cuckoo." Regis: "Is that your final answer?" Lisa: "Yes." Regis: "Are you confident?" Lisa: "Yes; I think Debbie's pretty smart." Regis: "You said C) cuckoo... And you're right! Congratulations, you have just won ONE MILLION DOLLARS!" To celebrate, Lisa flies Debbie to New York. That night they go out on the town. As they're sipping champagne, Lisa looks at Debbie and asks her," Tell me, how did you know that it was the cuckoo that does not build its own nest?" "Lisa, it was easy," replies Debbie. "Everybody knows that cuckoos live in clocks."

Apple-Cinnamon Crisp
"Adam Crisped Evie"

2	medium apples, peeled, sliced
2	Tablespoons red cinnamon candies
$^{1}/_{2}$	cup hot water
$^{3}/_{4}$	cup sugar
$^{1}/_{2}$	cup flour
4	Tablespoons margarine, melted

Place apple slices in pam-sprayed 8x8 baking dish.
Sprinkle candies on top of apples.
Pour hot water over candies.
Combine last 3 ingredients together.
Pour over apple mixture.
Bake at 375 degrees for 30 minutes.

Banana Buttermilk Salad
"Wanda's Monkeying Around"

1	cup sugar
1	cup buttermilk
4	bananas, mashed
1	(8 ounce) can crushed pineapple, drained
$^{1}/_{2}$	cup pecans, chopped
1	(8 ounce) frozen whipped topping

Combine all ingredients together.
Place in 9x9 dish.
Freeze.

Apple Cream Squares
"Wanna Cream Ed"

2   **cups self-rising flour**
2   **cups brown sugar**
1   **stick margarine, melted**
1   **cup pecans, chopped**
2   **teaspoons cinnamon**
1   **(8 ounce) sour cream**
1   **teaspoon vanilla**
1   **egg, beaten**
1   **medium apple, peeled, chopped**

Mix 1st 3 ingredients together until crumbly.
Stir in pecans.
Press 2¾ cups of mixture into pam-sprayed 9x13 baking dish.
Add rest of crumb mixture to last 5 ingredients.
Pour mixture over crumb crust.
Bake at 350 degrees for 25-35 minutes.

Apricot-Pineapple Freeze
"Ruby Redhead"

2 cups sugar
1 cup water
1 (16 ounce) bag frozen strawberries, thawed
1 (20 ounce) can crushed pineapple
1 (29 ounce) can apricots, drained, chopped
4 bananas, chopped

Combine 1st 2 ingredients in saucepan.
Simmer for 5 minutes.
Mix all ingredients together.
Spoon into foiled cupcake containers.
Freeze until firm.

Banana Pudding
"Moore Monkey Puddin'"

2 cups milk
1 small box French vanilla pudding
1 (14 ounce) can condensed milk
1 (12 ounce) frozen whipped topping
1 (12 ounce) box vanilla wafers
5 ripe bananas, sliced

Mix 1st 4 ingredients together.
Layer wafers, bananas and pudding in 9x13 dish.
Chill.

Blueberry Crunch
"Kaptain Kirk Krunch"

1   (20 ounce) can crushed pineapple
1   box yellow cake mix
3   cups fresh or frozen blueberries
$^{1}/_{2}$ cup sugar
1   stick margarine, melted
1   cup pecans, chopped

Spread pineapple in pam-sprayed 9x13 baking dish.
Layer next 3 ingredients in order given.
Drizzle with butter and **top** with pecans.
Bake at 350 degrees for 45 minutes.

Frozen Fruit Freeze
"MF Fruit Cake"

8   bananas, chopped
1   (12 ounce) can 7-up
2   (11 ounce) can mandarin oranges, chopped
1   (20 ounce) can crushed pineapple, drained
2   cups sugar
2   pints fresh strawberries, chopped
1   (6 ounce) can frozen lemon juice, thawed
1   (6 ounce) can frozen orange juice, thawed
1   (6 ounce) can frozen pink lemonade, thawed

Mix all ingredients together.
Spoon into foiled cupcake containers.
Freeze.

Hot Spiced Fruit
"Jay Bird's Paradise"

1	**(29 ounce) can pear halves, drained**
1	**(20 ounce) can sliced pineapple, drained**
1	**(16 ounce) can apricot halves, drained**
1	**(11 ounce) can mandarin oranges, drained**
1	**stick margarine**
1	**cup brown sugar**
1	**teaspoon cinnamon**
$^1/_8$	**teaspoon ground cloves**
$^1/_8$	**teaspoon vanilla**

Combine 1st 4 ingredients in 2 quart baking dish.
Combine last 5 ingredients in saucepan.
Stir over low heat, until margarine is melted.
Pour over fruit.
Bake at 325 degrees for 30 minutes.

Fly Me To The Moon

Once there was a **blonde** who was going to take flying lessons, so she went to the airport to rent a plane. The manager told her there were no planes left so she would have to use a helicopter. So the **blonde** got in the helicopter and took off. Every 10 miles she checked in with the manager; after the first 10 miles, she said it was a blast. When she reached 20 miles she told him that she had never seen so many buttons. But when she reached 30 miles she didn't check in so the manager went to rescue her. When he found her he asked her how she crashed. The **blonde** replied, "It was getting cold so I turned off the big fan."

Numbered Fruit Salad
"Your Days Are Numbered"

1 handful flaked coconut, toasted
2 Tablespoons frozen orange juice
3 orange sections
4 apple slices
5 cubes of cheddar cheese
6 banana slices
7 peach slices
8 seedless grapes
9 strawberries, sliced

Count each ingredient into bowl. **Stir** 9 times.

Strawberry Margarita Squares
"Gretch En Shots"

1 (16 ounce) frozen whole strawberries, halved
1/4 cup lime juice
2 Tablespoons tequila
2 Tablespoons Triple-Sec
6 cups vanilla ice cream, softened
20 unsalted pretzel sticks, crushed

Combine first 5 ingredients.
Pour into pam-sprayed 9x13 inch dish.
Sprinkle with pretzels.
Cover and **freeze** until firm.

Kiwi Fruit Pizza
"Lind See Your Fruit"

1 (20 ounce) sugar cookie dough
1 (8 ounce) cream cheese, softened
$^1/_2$ cup sugar
1 (8 ounce) frozen whipped topping
1 teaspoon vanilla
6 kiwi fruit, peeled, sliced
1 (16 ounce) can pineapple tidbits, drained
2 pints fresh strawberries, sliced
2 (11 ounce) cans mandarin oranges, drained

Press cookie dough on pam-sprayed pizza pan.
Bake at 350 degrees for 8-10 minutes.
Combine next 4 ingredients together.
Spread over cooled cookie.
Arrange fruit over cream cheese layer of cookie.
Refrigerate until ready to serve.

Blonde's Working!

Chelsea, a **blonde**, needed some extra cash, so she begged her friend at the highway department for a job – any job at all.

"Sure," he said. "I always have job openings to paint the lines down the center of the roads. Would you be interested in painting stripes?"

Chelsea agreed and began working immediately. The first day she painted five miles of stripes. The next day she painted three miles. But on the third day, she only painted one mile of stripes.

The supervisor took Chelsea aside and asked her what was wrong. "You worked so hard and painted so fast the first couple of days. Why are you working so slowly now?"

Chelsea replied, "Because the bucket keeps getting farther away."

Peach Delight
"Blonde Peach Fuzz"

$^1/_4$	cup flaked coconut
1	box white cake mix
$^1/_2$	stick margarine, melted
1	(16 ounce) can sliced peaches, drained
2	teaspoons sugar
$^1/_2$	teaspoon cinnamon
$^1/_2$	cup sour cream
1	egg, beaten
1	teaspoon vanilla

Combine 1st 3 ingredients together until crumbly.
Press mixture in pam-sprayed 9x13 baking dish.
Bake at 350 degrees for 10-15 minutes.
Arrange peaches over crust.
Sprinkle with sugar and cinnamon.
Blend last 3 ingredients.
Spread over top.
Bake at 350 degrees for 10 minutes.

A Blonde Needing Tech Support

Blonde: "Now what do I do?"
Tech Support: "What is the prompt on the screen?"
Blonde: "It's asking for 'Enter Your Last Name.' "
Tech Support: "Okay, so type in your last name."
Blonde: "How do you spell that?"

On The Grill

On The Grill

The Helpful Blonde

A **blonde** motorist was two hours from Jackson Mississippi when she was flagged down by a man whose truck had broken down. The man walked up to the car and asked, "Are you going to Jackson?" "Sure," answered the **blonde**, "Do you need a lift?" "Not for me. I'll be spending the next three hours fixing my truck. My problem is I've got two chimpanzees in the back which have to be delivered to the Jackson Zoo. They're a bit stressed already so I don't want to keep them on the road all day. Could you possibly take them to the zoo for me? I'll give you fifty dollars for your trouble." "I'd be happy to," said the **blonde**.

So the two chimpanzees were ushered into the back seat of the **blonde's** car and carefully strapped into their seat belts. Off they went. Five hours later, the truck driver was driving through the heart of Jackson when suddenly he was horrified!! There was the **blonde** walking down the street and holding hands with the two chimps. With a screech of brakes he pulled off the road and ran over to the **blonde**. "What the heck are you doing here?" he demanded, "I gave you fifty dollars to take these chimpanzees to the zoo." "Yes, I know you did," said the **blonde**, "But we had money left over—-so we went to the movies!!!"

Grilled Parmesan Asparagus
"Land On, Oh Spare Us"

15	stalks of fresh asparagus
2	Tablespoons olive oil
$1/2$	teaspoon salt
$1/2$	teaspoon Blonde Lemon-Pepper
$1/2$	cup Parmesan cheese
1	lemon, cut in wedges

Cut hard part of the asparagus bottoms off.
Place on aluminum foil.
Drizzle olive oil on asparagus.
Sprinkle with salt and lemon pepper.
Grill for 15-20 minutes. **Turn** occasionally.
Sprinkle with Parmesan cheese.
Grill for 5-10 more minutes.
Serve with lemon wedges.

Don't Panic

A **blonde** was on a flight from New York to Paris. Soon after take-off the pilot announces: "I'm sorry, but we have lost one of our engines. Subsequently, we will arrive in Paris approximately half an hour late." A few minutes later, he comes on again: "Hate to disappoint you folks, but another engine is down. Don't panic - we've still got two going, but now we'll be about 2 hours late." After another few minutes, he comes on again: "Look, I am really sorry about this, but somehow we have lost our third engine. Still nothing serious to worry about, but we will be about five hours late to Paris." After hearing this, the **blonde** turns to the guy sitting next to him and remarks, "If we lose the other one, we'll be up here all night."

Grilled Vidalia Onions
"Pearly Breath"

4	large Vidalia onions, skinned, rinsed
4	teaspoons margarine, divided into 4^{ths}
4	beef bouillon cubes
1/4	teaspoon Blonde All-Purpose Seasoning
1/4	teaspoon pepper
1/4	teaspoon salt

Place each onion on heavy-duty foil.
Cut a hole out in the center of each onion.
Place next 2 ingredients in center of each onion.
Sprinkle with last 3 ingredients.
Seal foil. **Grill** for 40-50 minutes.

Pizza Burgers
"Flipping For An Italian"

1	pound ground chuck
1	onion, finely chopped
1	(8 ounce) can pizza sauce
1	teaspoon garlic powder
1	teaspoon oregano
1	(8 ounce) shredded pizza cheese

Mix all ingredients together.
Shape into patties.
Grill, **flipping** occasionally.
Serve on hamburger buns.

Grilled Beef Coffee Can
"Blonde Man's Liquid Brain Brew"

1	potato, quartered
1	carrot, quartered
$1/2$	bell pepper, quartered
$1/4$	pound ground chuck
	Salt & pepper to taste
$1/2$	cup tomato juice

Line 1 pound coffee can with aluminum foil.
Layer 1st 4 ingredients in can. **Add** salt & pepper to each layer.
Add tomato juice.
Fold foil over top, **covering** tightly.
Place can on grill over medium heat.
Grill for 1 hour or until done.

Drivers!!

One day while a **blonde** was out driving her car, she ran into a truck. The truck driver made her pull over into a parking lot and get out of the car. He took a piece of chalk and drew a circle on the pavement. He told her to stand in the middle and not leave the circle. Furious, he went over to her car and slashed the tires. The **blonde** started laughing. This made the man angrier so he smashed her windshield. This time the **blonde** laughed even harder. Livid, the man broke all her windows and keyed her car. The **blonde** is now laughing hysterically, so the truck driver asks her what's so funny. The **blonde** giggled and replied, "When you weren't looking, I stepped out of the circle three times."

On The Grill

Grilled Steak Dinner
"Grilling A Chunk For TJ"

1   **chuck steak, 1 inch thick**
1   **package dry onion soup mix**
4   **potatoes, quartered**
4   **ribs of celery, quartered**
1   **bell pepper, quartered**
    Salt & pepper to taste

Place steak in center of heavy-duty aluminum foil.
Sprinkle with soup mix.
Cover with next 3 ingredients.
Sprinkle with salt & pepper.
Fold foil over leaving space for steam.
Place on grill over medium heat.
Grill for 1 hour or until done.

Survivor!

A **blonde**, a brunette and a redhead are all stuck on a deserted island together. The island is 20 miles from the nearest inhabited island so they all decide to try to swim there. The redhead makes it 10 miles, is exhausted, gives up, and drowns. The brunette makes it 15 miles before she's too tired to go any farther and drowns. The **blonde** gets 19 miles away from the deserted island, decides she's too tired to go any farther, and swims all the way back to the deserted island.

Barbecue Chicken
"Cued Breasts"

2   teaspoons Blonde Lemon-Pepper
2   teaspoons Blonde All-Purpose Seasoning
4   chicken breasts, boneless, skinless
2   teaspoons hot sauce
2   teaspoons Worcestershire
2   cups barbecue sauce

Sprinkle 1st 2 ingredients on chicken breasts.
Place chicken on grill, wrapped in foil.
Grill for 30 minutes or until done.
Mix last 3 ingredients together.
Baste both sides of chicken with sauce.
Grill for 5 more minutes.

Juicy Chicken
"Juicy Chick"

1   cup orange juice
1/3   cup lemon juice
1/4   cup oil
2   teaspoons soy sauce
2   teaspoons Italian seasoning
4   chicken breasts, boneless, skinless

Combine 1st 5 ingredients together.
Place chicken in marinade for 2-3 hours.
Grill for 30 minutes, **basting** occasionally.

On The Grill

Margarita Chicken
"Drunk Chick"

$1/4$	cup frozen limeade, thawed
$1/4$	cup tequila
2	Tablespoons Triple Sec
2	Tablespoons cilantro, chopped
$1/2$	(4 ounce) can diced jalapeños
4	chicken breasts, boneless, skinless

Combine 1st 5 ingredients together.
Place chicken in marinade in zip-lock bag.
Marinate in refrigerator for 2-3 hours.
Place chicken on grill.
Grill for 30 minutes, **basting** occasionally.

Lemon Pork Chops
"Peg's Puckered Up"

1	(6 ounce) can frozen lemonade, thawed
$2/3$	cup soy sauce
$1/2$	teaspoon garlic salt
$1/2$	teaspoon celery salt
$1/2$	teaspoon Blonde Lemon-Pepper
4	medium-size pork chops

Combine 1st 5 ingredients together.
Place pork chops in marinate for 2-3 hours.
Place pork on grill.
Grill for 15-20 minutes, **basting** occasionally.

Italian-Barbequed Spareribs
"Oh! Adam Spare Me The Rib"

1	**package dry Italian dressing mix**
2	**teaspoons Worcestershire**
³/₄	**cup ketchup**
1	**teaspoon chili powder**
1	**cup water**
3	**pounds spareribs, cut into serving pieces**

Mix 1ˢᵗ 5 ingredients together.
Place ribs in marinade for 2-3 hours.
Grill for 15-20 minutes, **basting** occasionally.

Grilled Tuna (ANY FISH)
"Bryant Blonde?"

2	**teaspoons olive oil**
2	**teaspoons lemon juice**
2	**teaspoons prepared horseradish**
2	**teaspoons prepared mustard**
2	**teaspoons garlic powder**
1	**pound tuna filets**

Combine 1ˢᵗ 5 ingredients together.
Place tuna in marinade.
Cover grill with foil. **Punch** holes in foil.
Place tuna on grill.
Turn tuna and **brush** with remaining marinade.
Grill until tuna flakes easily.

Shrimp & Scallop Kabobs
"Bill E Scalloped Me"

1   **(16 ounce) bottle Catalina French dressing**
2   **teaspoons Worcestershire**
2   **teaspoons garlic salt**
2   **teaspoons Blonde Lemon-Pepper**
2   **dashes hot sauce**
1   **pound shrimp, peeled**
1   **pound scallops**
1   **onion, quartered**
1   **bell pepper, quartered**

Mix 1st 5 ingredients together.
Add last 4 ingredients to marinade.
Marinate for 2-3 hours.
Thread shrimp, scallops, onion & pepper on skewers.
Cover grill rack with foil. **Punch** holes in foil.
Place skewers on foil.
Grill with lid down for 5-10 minutes.
Turn and **baste** occasionally with reserved marinade.

A Blonde Burglarized!

Returning home from work, a young **blonde** woman was shocked to find that her house had been ransacked and burglarized. She telephoned the police at once and reported the crime. The police dispatcher broadcasted the call on all channels and a K-9 unit patrolling nearby was the first to respond. As the K-9 officer approached the house with his dog on a leash. The **blonde** woman ran out on he porch and shuddered at the sight of the cop and his dog. Then she sat down on the steps, put her face in her hands and moaned, "I came home to find all my possessions stolen. I called the police for help, and what do they do? They send me a BLIND policeman!"

At Happy Hour

(Beverages)

At Happy Hour
(Beverages)

Standing Up

Falling Down

Outnumbered

A blind guy on a bar stool shouts to the bartender, "Wanna hear a **blonde** joke?"

In a hushed voice, the guy next to him says, "Before you tell that joke, you should know something."

"Our bartender is **blonde**, the bouncer is **blonde**. I'm a 6' tall, 200 lb. black belt. The guy sitting next to me is 6'2", weighs 225 and he's a rugby player. The fella to your right is 6'5" pushing 300 and he's a wrestler. Each one of us is **blonde**. Think about it, Mister. Do you still wanna tell that joke?"

The blind guy says, "Nah, not if I'm gonna have to explain it five times."

Juicy Punch
"Juicy Redhead"

1 quart apple juice
1 quart cranberry juice
1 (6 ounce) can frozen lemonade, thawed
2 cups water
1 cup sugar
1 liter ginger ale

Mix 1st 5 ingredients together and **freeze**.
Pour ginger ale over punch when ready to serve.

Leprechaun Punch
"The Luck Of Dakota"

1 small box lime gelatin
1 cup boiling water
1 (6 ounce) can frozen limeade, thawed
1 (6 ounce) can frozen lemonade, thawed
1 quart orange juice
1 quart pineapple juice
1 Tablespoon almond extract
2 drops green food coloring
1 liter ginger ale, chilled

Dissolve 1st 2 ingredients together.
Add next 6 ingredients. **Chill**.
Add ginger ale when ready to serve.

Orange Punch
"Stomping My Punch"

8	cups boiling water
1	large box orange gelatin
2	quarts orange juice
2	quarts pineapple juice
2	teaspoons vanilla
1	(6 ounce) can frozen lemonade, thawed

Combine all ingredients together.

Cranberry Tea
"Brown Sugar Blonde"

1	quart cranberry juice
1	quart pineapple juice
4	cups water
1	cup brown sugar
$1/8$	teaspoon ground cloves
$1/8$	teaspoon cinnamon

Combine all ingredients in large saucepan.
Simmer for 20 minutes.
Serve hot or cold.

Q: What does a blonde and a beer bottle have in common?
A: They're both empty from the neck up.

At Happy Hour
(Beverages)
(Standing Up)

Ginger Ale Iced Tea
"Aleing Chel"

8	cups boiling water
2	family size tea bags
1	cup sugar
1	(12 ounce) can frozen lemonade, thawed
2	teaspoons almond extract
1	liter ginger ale

Combine 1st 2 ingredients in saucepan.
Cover and steep for 15 minutes.
Remove tea bags, **squeeze** excess tea.
Add next 3 ingredients. **Chill**.
Add ginger ale when ready to serve.

Tropical Tea Cooler
"Walk Her To The Cooler"

1/3	cup sugar
3	Tablespoons instant tea
4 1/2	cups water
3	(12 ounce) cans apricot nectar
3	(6 ounce) cans frozen lemonade, thawed
6	(12 ounce) cans sprite

Combine 1st 3 ingredients until sugar dissolves.
Add remaining ingredients.

Bourbon Slush
"Gillespie's Slushed"

1/2	cup sugar
2	cups unsweetened tea
1	(6 ounce) can frozen lemonade, thawed
3/4	cup orange juice
6	cups water
2	cups Bourbon

Mix all ingredients together.
Freeze.
Scoop out when ready to serve.

Brandy Slush
"Mark It Slushed"

7	cups water
1¹/2	cups sugar
1	(12 ounce) can frozen lemonade, thawed
1	(12 ounce) can frozen orange juice, thawed
2	cups brandy
	Sprite

Mix 1st 4 ingredients together.
Add brandy. **Freeze**.
Scrape into glass, **mixing** 1/2 slush to 1/2 Sprite.

> **Q: What's a blondes' favorite rock group?**
> **A:** Air Supply.

At Happy Hour
(Beverages)
(Falling Down)

Champagne Punch
"Punched Out Blonde"

2   (10 ounce) bags frozen strawberries
1   quart vanilla ice cream
1   pint orange sherbet
1   (46 ounce) can pineapple juice
2   liters ginger ale
1   bottle pink champagne

Place frozen strawberries on bottom of punch bowl.
Add next 4 ingredients.
Stir in champagne before serving.

Bloody Mary on a Stick
"Mary Got Sticked Up"

Cherry tomatoes
Celery, quartered
Tomato juice
Celery salt
Vodka
Cocktail toothpicks

Put 1st 5 ingredients each in a separate bowl.
Put tomatoes & celery on toothpick.
Dip in tomato juice, salt & Vodka.
Eat tomato & celery off stick.
Don't get drunk.

85

At Happy Hour
(Beverages)
(Falling Down)

Grapetini
"Blondetini Bikini"

1 (6 ounce) can frozen orange juice, thawed
1 (6 ounce) can frozen grape juice, thawed
1 (6 ounce) can frozen lemonade, thawed
1 can vodka
1 (12 ounce) can Sprite
Grapes for garnishing

Mix 1st 5 ingredients together.
Serve over ice. **Garnish** with grapes.

Rum Tea
"Rummed Reynolds"

2 cups rum
2/3 cup sugar
1 cup orange juice
1/4 cup lemon juice
1/4 cup vodka
4 cups hot tea, strong

Combine 1st 2 ingredients in saucepan.
Bring to a boil.
Stir in remaining ingredients. **Simmer**.
Serve over ice.

In Italy

(Italian Food)

In Italy
(Italian Food)

Blonde on Board

A plane is on its way to Houston when a **blonde** in economy class gets up and moves to the first class section and sits down. The flight attendant watches her do this and asks to see her ticket. She then tells the **blonde** that she paid for economy class and that she will have to sit in the back. The **blonde** replies, "I'm **blonde**, I'm beautiful, I'm going to Houston and I'm staying right here." The flight attendant goes into the cockpit and tells the pilot and the co-pilot that there is a **blonde** sitting in first class who belongs in economy and won't move back to her seat.

The co-pilot goes back to the **blonde** and tries to explain that because she only paid for economy she will have to leave and return to her seat. The **blonde** replies, "I'm **blonde**, I'm beautiful, I'm going to Houston and I'm staying right here." The co-pilot tells the pilot that he should probably have the police waiting when they land to arrest this **blonde** woman who won't listen to reason.

The pilot says, "You say she is a **blonde**? I'll handle this. I'm married to a **blonde**. I speak **blonde**." He goes back to the **blonde** and whispers in her ear, and she says, "Oh, I'm sorry." She gets up and goes back to her seat in economy. The flight attendant and co-pilot are amazed and asked him what he said to make her move without any fuss. "I told her first class isn't going to Houston."

Italian Spread
"Art You Glad You Didn't Spread"

2   (8 ounce) cream cheese, softened
1   (8 ounce) goat cheese
4   teaspoons oregano
1   (8.5 ounce) jar sun-dried tomatoes, chopped
1   (6 ounce) jar marinated artichoke hearts,
     chopped
1   (15 ounce) can heart of palm, chopped

Combine all ingredients together.
Serve with crackers.

Artichoke-Italian Salad
"Charm Him Chokin'"

1   (3 ounce) envelope plain gelatin
1   cup boiling water
1   cup mayonnaise
1   (14 ounce) can artichoke hearts, chopped
1   (10 ounce) bag frozen green peas
2   Tablespoons lemon juice
1   (4 ounce) jar diced pimientos, drained
1   (8 ounce) shredded mozzarella cheese
1   teaspoon Italian seasoning

Mix 1st 2 ingredients together until dissolved.
Combine all ingredients together.
Pour into ring mold and **refrigerate**.

89

Italian Rice Salad
"Leonardo Potpourri"

3	cups rice, cooked
1	(6 ounce) jar marinated artichoke hearts,
1	(4 ounce) can sliced ripe olives
2	ribs of celery, chopped
$^1/_2$	cup frozen green peas
$^1/_2$	cup Italian dressing

Combine all ingredients together.
Refrigerate over night.

Broccoli 3 Cheese Toss
"A Cheesy Toss"

1	(16 ounce) bag frozen broccoli spears
1	(8 ounce) ricotta cheese
1	(4 ounce) blue cheese, crumbled
1	(3 ounce) cream cheese, softened
$^2/_3$	cup milk
$^1/_2$	cup parsley

Steam the broccoli.
Combine next 3 ingredients until smooth.
Beat in milk. **Stir** in parsley.
Toss all ingredients together.

Q: A blonde ordered a pizza and the clerk asked if he should cut it in six or twelve pieces.
A: "Six, please. I could never eat twelve pieces."

Italian Wedding Soup
"Here Comes The Diago"

2	(46 ounce) cans chicken broth
1¹/₂	pounds ground beef
1	egg, beaten
¹/₂	teaspoon Italian seasoning
1	(10 ounce) frozen chopped spinach
1	teaspoon salt
1	teaspoon pepper
¹/₂	cup parmesan cheese
6	eggs, beaten

Heat broth in large soup pot.
Combine next 3 ingredients together.
Form into marble-sized balls.
Brown in skillet. **Drain.**
Add meatballs & spinach to broth.
Simmer for 20 minutes.
Add next 3 ingredients together.
While **stirring** soup in a circle **pour** in egg mixture.
Simmer for 10 more minutes.

You've Got Mail!

A man was trimming his bushes. His neighbor (a **blonde**) walks out, checks her mail only to see that it's empty, and goes back inside. Five minutes later, she comes back out, checks her mail again only to see that it's still empty, and goes back in. The third time she comes out, the man asks her, "Excuse me, is there a problem?" The **blonde** replies, "Darn right there's a problem! My computer keeps on telling me 'I've got mail'!"

Spinach Lasagna Roll-Ups
"It's All Rolled Up"

1	(16 ounce) lasagna noodles, cooked according to directions
1	package dry Ranch dressing
1	(8 ounce) cream cheese, softened
1	(10 ounce) frozen chopped spinach, thawed, drained
1	(8 ounce) can tomato sauce
3/4	cup milk
1	teaspoon salt
1	teaspoon Italian seasoning
1	(8 ounce) shredded mozzarella cheese

Arrange noodles in pam-sprayed 9x13 baking dish.
Combine next 2 ingredients together.
Mix half of this mixture with the spinach.
Spread 2 tablespoons of spinach mixture over each noodle.
Roll each noodle and **place** seam side down.
Combine next 4 ingredients with remaining mixture.
Pour over roll-ups. **Cover** with foil.
Bake at 325 degrees for 25 minutes.
Sprinkle with mozzarella cheese.
Cover loosely and **bake** 10 more minutes.

Q: Why do blondes always smile during lightning storms?
A: They think their picture is being taken.

In Italy
(Italian Food)

Zucchini Bake
"Cucurbitaceae Me"

2	medium zucchini, sliced
1	medium onion, sliced
1	tomato, sliced
1/2	teaspoon dried basil
1	teaspoon oregano
1	(16 ounce) can tomato sauce
2	slices of bread, buttered, cubed
1/2	cup grated parmesan cheese
	Salt & pepper to taste

Layer 1st 3 ingredients in pam-sprayed 9x13 pan.
Combine last 6 ingredients.
Pour over vegetables.
Bake at 350 degrees for 45-55 minutes.

A Blonde Interview

An executive was interviewing a nervous, young **blonde** woman for a position in his company.

He wanted to find out something about her personality so he asked, "If you could have a conversation with someone, living or dead, who would it be?"

The **blonde** quickly responded, "The living one."

Mozzarella Beef Pie
"Meating Is Cheesy"

1¹/₂   **pounds ground beef**
¹/₂   **onion, chopped**
2   **ribs of celery, chopped**
1   **(8 ounce) mozzarella cheese, divided**
1   **package dry spaghetti mix**
1   **(8 ounce) crescent rolls**

Brown beef. **Drain**.
Add next 2 ingredients, **cook** until tender.
Add ¹/₂ cup cheese and spaghetti mix
Put rolls in pam-sprayed 9x13 baking dish.
Pour meat mixture on rolls, **top** with remaining cheese.
Bake at 375 degrees for 15-20 minutes.

A Blonde Buying A TV!

A **blonde** went into an appliance store that was having a sale on TVs. She walked up to the counter and said to the clerk, "I would like to buy this TV."

The clerk replied, "Sorry, I don't sell to **blondes**."

So, the **blonde** dyed her hair brown and returned the next day. Again, she went up to the counter and said, "I would like to buy this TV."

And again, the clerk answered, "Sorry, I don't sell to **blondes**."

Puzzled, the **blonde** asked, "How did you know I was a **blonde**?"

And the clerk said, "Because that is a microwave."

Mozzarella Chicken
"Brew Her Harry"

$1/4$	cup olive oil
4	chicken breasts, boneless, skinless
$1/2$	cup Italian dressing
1	cup breadcrumbs
2	cups marinara sauce
4	slices of mozzarella cheese
1	tomato, chopped
2	teaspoons Italian seasoning
$1/2$	cup parmesan cheese

Heat olive oil in large frying pan.
Dip chicken in dressing, then in bread crumbs.
Brown in oil. **Place** in pam-spayed 9x13 baking dish.
Spoon marinara sauce over chicken.
Top with last 4 ingredients. **Cover** with foil.
Bake at 350 degrees for 1 hour & 15 minutes.

Mirror, Mirror, On The Wall!

A **blonde**, a brunette, and a redhead are standing in front of the mirror of truth. It sucks up and kills anyone who tells a lie in front of it. So the brunette says, "I'm the smartest person in the world." She gets sucked up and dies. The redhead says, "I've got the most curly hair," and she gets sucked up and dies also. The **blonde** says, "I think....." And she gets sucked up and dies.

In Italy
(Italian Food)

Cannoli Cream Pie
"Fertility Cream"

- 2 frozen pie shells
- 1 small box instant vanilla pudding
- 1 (8 ounce) cream cheese, softened
- 2 cups milk
- 1 pint whipping cream, whipped
- 1/2 teaspoon almond extract
- 1 (2.5 ounce) slivered almonds
- 1 (6 ounce) bag chocolate chips
- 1 (2 ounce) jar of cherries, chopped

Bake pie shell according to directions.
Mix next 5 ingredients together.
Add next 3 ingredients. **Mix** well.
Pour into both pie shells. **Refrigerate**.

Smart Thinking

A **blonde**, a redhead, and a brunette were driving through the desert when their car broke down. They decided they would all walk to civilization. The redhead said, "I'm going to take water so if I get thirsty I can drink it." Then the brunette said, "I'm going to take some food so if I get hungry I can eat." And then the **blonde** said "I'm going to take the car door, so if I get hot, I can roll the window down!"

Chocolate Italian Cream Cake
"That's A Brown Italian"

1	**box chocolate cake mix**
3	**eggs, beaten**
$^1/_3$	**cup vegetable oil**
1	**(16 ounce) carton ricotta cheese**
1	**cup sugar**
1	**teaspoon vanilla**
1	**small box instant chocolate pudding**
1	**(8 ounce) frozen whipped topping, thawed**
	Sprinkle of chocolate chips

Combine 1st 3 ingredients together.
Pour into pam-sprayed 9x13 baking dish.
Combine next 3 ingredients, **mixing** well.
Pour over cake batter, **swirl** with knife.
Bake at 350 degrees for 1 hour. Let **cool**.
Combine last 3 ingredients until smooth. **Refrigerate**.
Cover cake with pudding mixture. **Refrigerate**.

Salon Tale!

A **blonde** wearing headphones, walks into a hair salon to get her hair cut. The stylist asks her to take off her headphones but the **blonde** refuses. So the stylist takes them off and the **blonde** collapses to the ground and dies. The stylist picks up the headphones and hears, "Breathe in, breathe out. Breathe in, breathe out..."

Italian Chicken
"Spatchcock Italian-Style"

4   **chicken breasts, boneless, skinless**
1   **(4 ounce) cream cheese & chives**
1   **can cream of mushroom soup**
1   **package dry Italian seasoning mix**
1   **cup water**
     Salt & pepper to taste

Place chicken breasts in pam-sprayed 9x13 baking dish.
Combine last 5 ingredients together.
Pour over chicken. **Cover** with foil.
Bake at 350 degrees for 1 hour & 15 minutes.

Wishing!

A brunette, a redhead and a **blonde** are walking down a beach when suddenly the brunette discovers a magic lamp. The brunette rubs the lamp and poof! A magic genie appears. The genie tells the girls that he will grant them three wishes, so each girl will have a turn. The redhead goes first and tells the genie that she's always been really smart and she is sick of being teased, so she asks the genie to make her just semi-smart. Suddenly the redhead is turned into a brunette. Next, the brunette takes her turn. She tells the genie that she has always just been sort of smart and she wants to be really smart. Suddenly the brunette becomes a redhead. Finally, it's the **blonde's** turn. She thinks for a minute and then tells the genie that she's always been dumb and she's tired of being dumb. The **blonde** says that she wants to be really dumb. Suddenly, the **blonde** becomes a man!

With Junkfood

With Junkfood

Porch Painting!

A **blonde**, wanting to earn some money, decided to hire herself out as a handyman-type and started canvassing a wealthy neighborhood. She went to the front door of the first house and asked the owner if he had any jobs for her to do. "Well, you can paint my porch. How much will you charge?"

The **blonde** said "How about 50 dollars?" The man agreed and told her that the paint and other materials that she might need were in the garage. The man's wife heard the conversation and said to her husband, "Does she realize that the porch goes all the way around the house?" The man replied, "She should, she was standing on it."

A short time later, the **blonde** came to the door to collect her money. "You're finished already?" He asked. "Yes," the **blonde** answered, "And I had paint left over, so I gave it two coats." Impressed, the man reached in his pocket for the $50. ......"and by the way," the **blonde** added, "It's not a porch, it's a ferrari."

Cheddar Crackers
"Crack Hers"

1 stick margarine, softened
1 (16 ounce) shredded cheddar cheese
Cayenne pepper to taste
1 teaspoon oregano
1 envelope dry onion soup mix
1 cup all-purpose flour

Combine 1st 2 ingredients together.
Add last 4 ingredients.
Shape into 2 rolls, 1-inch thick.
Wrap in foil. **Chill** until firm.
Slice into 1/4 inch slices.
Place on cookie sheet.
Bake at 375 degrees for 10-12 minutes.

Critter Munch
"Tarty Critters"

1¹/₂ cups animal cracker cookies
1¹/₂ cups goldfish crackers
1 cup dried tart cherries
1 cup M&M's
1 cup honey roasted peanuts
1 cup Reeses pieces

Mix all ingredients together.

Cheese Twist Party Mix
"Twist & Score"

1	(16 ounce) box oyster crackers
1	(16 ounce) box cheese twists
1	envelope Italian salad dressing mix
1	Tablespoon dill weed
2	Tablespoons Blonde Lemon-Pepper
$1/2$	teaspoon red pepper
$1/2$	teaspoon garlic powder
$1/2$	teaspoon salt
1	cup oil

Mix 1st 2 ingredients in 9x13 baking pan.
Mix next 7 ingredients together.
Pour over crackers.
Bake at 350 degrees for 10 minutes. **Stirring** frequently.
Pour into brown paper bag. **Shake** well.
Store in airtight container.

Q: How do you keep a blonde busy?
A: Write, "Please turn over" on both sides of a piece of paper.

Hot Nuts
"Hot Cross Nuts"

2	**Tablespoons olive oil**
$^1/_2$	**teaspoon garlic salt**
$^1/_2$	**teaspoon ground cumin**
$^1/_2$	**teaspoon chili powder**
$^1/_4$	**teaspoon cinnamon**
$^1/_4$	**teaspoon curry powder**
$^1/_4$	**teaspoon ground red pepper**
2	**cups whole almonds**
2	**cups pecan halves**

Heat oil.
Stir in next 6 ingredients.
Add almonds & **stir**. **Add** pecans & **stir**.
Spread on cookie sheet.
Bake at 325 degrees for 15 minutes. **Stir** every 5 minutes.
Cool before serving.

Blondes Clapping!

There were eleven people hanging onto a rope that came down from an airplane. Ten were **blonde** and one was a brunette. They all decided that one person should get off because if they didn't, the rope would break and everyone would die.

No one could decide who should go, so finally the brunette said, "I'll get off."

After a really touching speech from the brunette saying she would get off, all of the **blondes** started clapping.

Mexican Munch
"High Dee Munch"

2	cups Cheerios cereal
4	cups corn Chex cereal
2	(3 ounce) cans French-fried onions
1	(7 ounce) can shoestring potatoes
1	(5 ounce) can chow mein noodles
1^1/$_2$	cups Spanish peanuts
1	(2.5 ounce) package slivered almonds
1	envelope taco seasoning mix
1	stick margarine, melted

Mix all ingredients together in large bowl.
Pour ^{1}/$_2$ mixture on cookie sheet.
Bake at 250 degrees for 30 minutes.
Stirring every 10 minutes.
Do other half of mixture.
Store in airtight container.

Q: Did you hear about the blonde who stood in front of a mirror with her eyes closed?
A: She wanted to see what she looked like asleep.

With Junkfood

Salty Mix
"A Blonde Mixer"

2	sticks margarine, melted
2	Tablespoons Worcestershire sauce
$^3/_4$	teaspoon garlic powder
$1^1/_2$	teaspoons seasoned salt
$^1/_2$	teaspoon onion powder
$^1/_2$	teaspoon Blonde All-Purpose Seasoning

Mix all ingredients together.

1	cup mixed nuts
1	cup mini pretzels
1	cup bagel chips
3	cups crispy corn cereal squares
3	cups crispy rice cereal squares
3	cups crispy wheat cereal squares

Mix all ingredients together.
Combine seasoning mixture and chip mixture together.
Store in airtight container.

Q: Why do men like blonde jokes?
A: Because they can understand them.

105

With Junkfood

Oat Munch
"Sticky & Munchy"

1 (16 ounce) box Oat cereal squares
2 cups whole pecans
1/2 cup corn syrup
1/2 cup brown sugar
1/2 stick margarine
1 teaspoon vanilla

Combine 1st 2 ingredients on a cookie sheet. **Set** aside.
Combine last 4 ingredients in microwaveable bowl.
Microwave on High 1 1/2 minutes. **Stir** & **turn** bowl.
Microwave on High 1 more minute or until **boiling**.
Pour over cereal mixture.
Bake at 250 degrees for 1 hour and 20 minutes.
Stir every 20 minutes. **Store** in airtight container.

Sweet Munch
"Gooey & Munchy"

1 pound white chocolate, melted
1 cup crunchy peanut butter
1 cup cocktail peanuts
1 cup Rice Krispies
1 cup mini-marshmallows, melted
1 teaspoon vanilla

Mix all ingredients together.
Drop by teaspoons on wax paper until set.

Pudding Peanuts
"Shakey Nuts"

1	**cup sugar**
1	**small box vanilla pudding, (not instant)**
¹/₂	**cup evaporated milk**
1	**Tablespoon margarine**
1	**cup salted peanuts**
¹/₄	**teaspoon vanilla**

Mix 1st 2 ingredients together in a saucepan.
Add next 2 ingredients.
Stir to a boil.
Lower heat stirring constantly for 3 minutes.
Remove from heat.
Add last 2 ingredients.
Stir until thick and creamy.
Drop by teaspoon onto wax paper to cool.

The Oinks Have It!

A **blonde** is walking down the street with a pig under her arm. She passes a person who asks "Where did you get that?" The pig says, "I won her in a raffle!"

Praline Nibbles
"Nibbles & Rigby"

1	**stick margarine**
³/₄	**cup brown sugar**
1	**cup pecans, broken**
2	**cups rice Chex cereal**
2	**cups corn Chex cereal**
2	**cups wheat Chex cereal**

Combine 1ˢᵗ 2 ingredients together in a saucepan.
Bring mixture to a boil over medium heat, **stirring** constantly.
Cook for 2 minutes.
Combine all ingredients together.
Place in pam-sprayed 9x13 baking dish.
Bake at 325 degrees for 8-10 minutes. **Stirring**.

Thoughts to Ponder

Man says to God, "Why did you make **blondes** so beautiful?"

God says, "So you would love her."

Man says to God, "Why did you make her so dumb?"

God says, "So she would love you."

Snicker Bar Delight
"Don't Snick Her! Mark Her!"

1   **(16 ounce) marshmallows**
1   **stick margarine**
1   **teaspoon vanilla**
5   **Snicker bars, cut up**
1   **(12 ounce) box Crispix**
1   **Snicker bar, finely chopped**

Combine 1st 4 ingredients in saucepan until melted.
Pour mixture over Crispix.
Press into pam-sprayed 9x13 dish.
Sprinkle last Snicker bar on top.

Holy Craps!

Two bored casino dealers were waiting at the craps table. A very attractive **blonde** woman arrived and bet twenty thousand dollars ($20,000) on a single roll of the dice. She said, "I hope you don't mind, but I feel much luckier when I'm completely nude." With that, she stripped from the neck down, rolled the dice and yelled, "Come on, baby, Mama needs new clothes!" As the dice came to a stop, she jumped up and down and squealed... "Yes! yes! I won, I won!" She hugged each of the dealers and then picked up her winnings and her clothes and quickly departed. The dealers stared at each other dumbfounded. Finally, one of them asked, "What did she roll?" The other answered, "I don't know - I thought you were watching."

Chocolate Twinkie Dessert
"Twinkle, Twinkle MiMi"

9	**Twinkies**
1	**large box instant chocolate pudding**
1¹/₂	**cups milk**
4	**cups vanilla ice cream (softened)**
1	**(8 ounce) frozen whipped topping, thawed**
3	**Heath candy bars, crushed** *(I put them into a large baggie, and pound with a mallet)*

Slice Twinkies lengthwise and **lay** in 9x13 pan, filling side up.
Mix next 3 ingredients together. **Spread** on top of Twinkies.
Top with last 2 ingredients.
Keep **refrigerated**.

Classic Burn Out!

I decided that I needed a few days off and I realized that I had run out of vacation time. I figured the best way to get the boss to send me home was to act a little crazy. I figured he'd think I was burning out and give me some time off. I went in to work early the next day and began hanging upside down from the ceiling. Just then one of my co-workers (she's **blonde**...it'll be important later) came in and asked me what I was doing. "Shh," I said, "I'm acting crazy to get a few days off. I'm a light bulb." A second later the boss walked by and asked me what I was doing. "I'm a light bulb!" I exclaimed. "You're going crazy," he said. "Take a few days off." With that, I jumped down and started walking out. The **blonde** started following me and the boss asked where she was going. "I can't work in the dark," she said.

With Kisses
(Sweets)

With Kisses
(Sweets)

A Blonde and Her Puzzle

A **blonde** calls her boyfriend and says, "Please come over here and help me. I have a killer jigsaw puzzle, and I can't figure out how to get it started." Her boyfriend asks, "What is it supposed to be when it's finished?" The **blonde** says, "According to the picture on the box, it's a tiger." Her boyfriend decides to go over and help with the puzzle. She lets him in and shows him where she has the puzzle spread all over the table. He studies the pieces for a moment, looks at the box, then turns to her and says, "First of all, no matter what we do, we're not going to be able to assemble these pieces into anything resembling a tiger." He takes her hand and says, "Second, I want you to relax. Let's have a nice cup of tea, and then....." He sighed, ... "Let's put all these frosted flakes back in the box."

Almond Joy Fudge Brownies
"Don't Fudge Joy"

1	box brownie mix
3	Tablespoons oil
1	(14 ounce) can condensed milk
1	(14 ounce) package miniature almond joy, chopped
1	(2 ounce) bag almonds
	Powdered sugar

Prepare brownie mix according to directions, using only 3 Tablespoons of oil.

Pour into pam-sprayed 9x13 baking dish.

Pour condensed milk over batter.

Sprinkle with next 2 ingredients.

Bake at 350 for 35-40 minutes.

Cool completely before cutting into squares.

Sprinkle with powdered sugar.

Blonde Eye Glasses

A **blonde** went to an eye doctor to have her eyes checked for glasses. The doctor directed her to read various letters with the left eye while covering the right eye. The **blonde** was so mixed up on which eye was which that the eye doctor, in disgust, took a paper bag with a hole in it to see through, covered up the appropriate eye, and asked her to read the letters. As he did so, he noticed the **blonde** had tears streaming down her face. "Look," said the doctor, "There's no need to get emotional about getting glasses."

"I know," agreed the **blonde**, "But I kind of had my heart set on wire frames.

Cake Pecan Bars
"Cakey Not Flakey"

1	box yellow cake mix, with pudding
2	eggs, beaten
1	stick margarine, melted
1	cup pecans, chopped
1	(8 ounce) cream cheese, softened
1	stick margarine, melted
1/2	teaspoon vanilla
2	eggs, beaten
1	(16 ounce) box powdered sugar

Combine 1st 4 ingredients together.
Press into pam-sprayed 9x13 baking dish.
Mix last 5 ingredients together thoroughly.
Press on top of 1st mixture.
Bake at 325 degrees for 1 hour.
Cool completely before cutting into squares.

Emergency

A **blonde** comes home from a day of shopping and discovers that her house is on fire, so she calls the fire department on her cell phone.

"Please state the nature of your emergency," says the operator.

"Help! My house is on fire!" The **blonde** replies.

"Okay, Where do you live?"

"In a house you silly billy!" The **blonde** replies.

"No, No! How do we get there?" The operator asks frustratedly.

"Duh! Big red truck!!"

With Kisses
(Sweets)

Gooey Turtle Bars
"Slow & Gooey"

1	stick margarine, melted
1¹/₂	cups vanilla wafer crumbs
1	(12 ounce) bag chocolate chips
1	(6 ounce) bag butterscotch chips
1	cup pecans, chopped
1	(12 ounce) jar caramel topping

Combine 1ˢᵗ 2 ingredients.
Press into pam-sprayed 9x13 baking dish.
Sprinkle with next 3 ingredients.
Remove lid from caramel topping and **heat** in microwave 1 to 1¹/₂ minutes, **stirring** every 30 seconds.
Drizzle over chips & pecans.
Bake at 350 degrees for 12–15 minutes.
Chill at least 30 minutes before cutting.

Highway Signs

A police officer pulls over a car with a young **blonde** driver in it.
Cop: "Miss, this is a 65 MPH highway, why are you going so slow?"
Blonde: "Officer, I saw a lot of signs saying 22, not 65."
Cop: "Oh, Miss, that's not the speed limit, that's the name of the highway you're on!"
Blonde: "Oh! Stupid me! Thanks for letting me know, I'll be more careful from now on."
At this point the cop looks into the back seat of the car where the passengers are shaking and white as ghosts.
Cop: "Excuse me Miss, what's wrong with your friends back there? They're shaking something awful."
Blonde: "Oh… We just got off highway 119."

115

Bourbon Pound Cake
"Comstock's Pounding"

1	**box vanilla cake mix**
³/₄	**cup water**
¹/₃	**cup vegetable oil**
2	**eggs, beaten**
¹/₂	**cup bourbon**
	powdered sugar

Combine 1ˢᵗ 5 ingredients together.
Pour in pam-sprayed bundt pan.
Bake at 350 degrees for 50-60 minutes.
Sprinkle with powdered sugar.

Key-Lime Cheesecake
"Billy Bob's Limey"

3	**eggs, beaten**
2	**(8 ounce) cream cheese, softened**
²/₃	**cup sugar**
1	**(16 ounce) carton sour cream**
¹/₄	**cup key lime juice**
1	**(9-inch) deep-dish graham cracker crust**

Beat 1ˢᵗ 5 ingredients until creamy. **Pour** into piecrust.
Bake at 350 degrees for 60-70 minutes.
Cool in refrigerator before serving.

Raspberry Chocolate Cake
"Razzle Dazzle His Cake"

1   **box chocolate cake mix**
1   **(10 ounce) bag frozen raspberries, thawed**
1   **(8 ounce) sour cream**
4   **Tablespoons Blonde Raspberry Honey Jelly**
$^1/_2$ **cup water**
3   **eggs, beaten**

Combine all ingredients together.
Pour in pam-sprayed bundt pan.
Bake at 325 degrees for 50-60 minutes.

Southern Cream Cookies
"Southern Creamy Girly"

1   **cup Crisco**
2   **cups sugar**
3   **eggs, beaten**
1   **teaspoon vanilla**
1   **(8 ounce) sour cream**
5   **cups self-rising flour**

Cream 1st 2 ingredients together.
Add next 3 ingredients. **Mix** well.
Add flour making a stiff dough.
Drop by teaspoonfuls on cookie sheet.
Press down with fork.
Bake at 350 degrees for 12-15 minutes.

Almond Joy Cookie
"Martin's Minked & Aired"

2 (1 ounce) squares unsweetened chocolate
1 (14 ounce) can condensed milk
3 cups sweetened flaked coconut
1 teaspoon vanilla extract
1 pinch salt
1 (2 ounce) bag whole almonds

Melt 1st 2 ingredients together in double boiler. **Stirring**.
Pour the melted chocolate over coconut.
Stir in the vanilla and salt. **Mix** well.
Drop by teaspoonfuls on cookie sheet with parchment paper.
Press one whole almond into the top of each cookie.
Bake at 350 degrees for 10-12 minutes.
Check at 8 minutes as the bottoms tend to burn easily.
Remove from oven and cool.

A Popsicle Blonde

A **blonde** was shopping and came across a silver thermos. She was quite fascinated by it, so she picked it up and took it over to the clerk to ask what it was. The clerk said, "Why, that's a thermos ... it keeps things hot and some things cold."

"Wow," said the **blonde**, "That's amazing ... I'm going to buy it!" So she bought the thermos and took it to work the next day. Her boss saw it on her desk. "What's that?" he asked. "Why, that's a thermos ... it keeps hot things hot and cold things cold," she replied.

Her boss inquired, "What do you have in it now?" The **blonde** replied ... "Two frozen popsicles and some hot coffee."

Fruit Cocktail Cookies
"Fruity Cock Tails"

1	**cup Crisco**
1	**cup brown sugar**
1/2	**cup sugar**
3	**eggs, beaten**
2	**cups fruit cocktail, chopped, with juice**
1	**cup pecans, chopped**
1	**teaspoon vanilla**
4	**cups self-rising flour**
1/2	**teaspoon cinnamon**

Cream 1st 3 ingredients together.
Add next 6 ingredients. **Mix** well.
Drop by teaspoonfuls on cookie sheet.
Bake at 375 degrees for 12-15 minutes.

Frozen Pumpkin Pie
"Anything You Want Punkin?"

1	**cup canned pumpkin**
1	**cup brown sugar**
1/2	**teaspoon salt**
1/2	**teaspoon cinnamon**
1	**quart vanilla ice cream, softened**
2	**(9 inch) graham cracker pie crusts**

Mix 1st 5 ingredients together until creamy.
Pour mixture into 2 pie crusts.
Place pies in freezer for 3 hours.

Sherbet Pie
"Sure Pam!"

1   (8 ounce) cream cheese, softened
1   (7 ounce) jar marshmallow crème
2   cups orange sherbet, softened
1   (8 ounce) frozen whipped topping, thawed
1   (9 inch) deep-dish graham cracker crust
1   orange, sliced for garnish

Beat 1st 2 ingredients together until smooth.
Stir in next 2 ingredients.
Pour into crust.
Freeze for 3 hours.
Garnish with orange slices.
Remove from freezer 10 minutes before serving.

Peach Pie
"Isn't She Such A Peach?"

1   (8 ounce) cream cheese, softened
1   cup powdered sugar
1/4   teaspoon almond extract
3/4   cup whipping cream, whipped
1   (16 ounce) can sliced peaches, drained
1   (9 inch) deep-dish graham cracker crust

Cream 1st 3 ingredients together.
Fold in next 2 ingredients.
Pour filling into crust.
Chill before serving.

In Louisiana

(Cajun Food)

In Louisiana
(Cajun Food)

You Might Be A Blonde Cajun If...

...you start an angel food cake with a roux.

...you think a lobster is a crawfish on steroids.

...you think ground hog day and boucherie day are the same holiday.

...you take a bite of 5-alarm Texas chili and reach for the Tabasco.

...you pass up a trip abroad to go to the crawfish festival in Breaux Bridge.

...your children's favorite bedtime story begins, "First you make a roux..."

...your description of a gourmet dinner includes the words "deep fat fried."

...your mama announces each morning, "Well, I've got the rice cooking—what will we have for dinner?"

...you sit down to eat boiled crawfish and your host says, "Don't eat the dead ones," and you know what he means.

...you don't know the real names of your friends, only their nicknames.

...you gave up Tabasco for Lent.

...you know the difference between Zatarains and zydeco.

...your dog thinks the bed of your pickup is his kennel.

...all of your dessert recipes call for jalapeños.

...you think the four seasons are: duck, rabbit, deer, and squirrel.

Louisiana Cheese Ball
"Blonde Tod Ball"

$1/2$	cup sour cream
$1/2$	cup mayonnaise
1	Tablespoon lemon juice
1	Tablespoon hot sauce
4	green onions, chopped
1	(16 ounce) shredded jalapeño cheese

Mix all ingredients together.
Serve with crackers.

Artichoke-Shrimp Creole Salad
"Chokin' For Freddy"

1	pound crawfish tails
1	lemon, juice
1	teaspoon Blonde Lemon Pepper
$1/2$	teaspoon creole seasoning
1	(5.5 ounce) jar creole mustard
$1/2$	cup ketchup
2	Tablespoons horseradish
1	(14 ounce) can artichoke hearts, chopped
$1/2$	cup capers

Sauté 1st 4 ingredients together.
Combine all ingredients together.
Refrigerate to chill.

Creole White Bean Soup
"Lovejoy Beans"

1/4	cup minced onion
2	ribs of celery, chopped
1/2	bell pepper, chopped
2	Tablespoons margarine
1	pound smoked sausage, 1/2 inch slices
1	(8 ounce) can tomato sauce
2	(16 ounce) navy white beans with bacon
4	cups water
	Salt & pepper to taste

Sauté 1st 4 ingredients together until tender.
Add next 2 ingredients. **Simmer** 15-20 minutes.
Add last 3 ingredients. **Simmer** for 30 minutes.

Cajun Potatoes
"Bubba's Studding"

4	potatoes, peeled, sliced thin
1	(8 ounce) shredded cheddar cheese
1/2	stick butter, sliced
	Seasoning to taste
	Salt & pepper to taste
1	can cream of chicken soup

Layer all ingredients in order given in pam-sprayed 9x13 pan.
Bake at 350 degrees for 1 hour.

Crawfish & Cream Cheese Soup
"He Crawfished Her"

1	(8 ounce) cream cheese, softened
1	stick margarine
3	green onions, chopped
2	cans cream of potato soup
1	(15 ounce) can shoe peg corn
1	(15 ounce) can cream-style corn
2	cups milk
1	teaspoon creole seasoning
1	pound crawfish tails, cooked

Melt 1st 2 ingredients slowly in a large pot.
Add green onions. **Simmer** for 15 minutes.
Add next 3 ingredients. **Cook** for 15 minutes.
Add milk ½ cup at a time. **Stirring** slowly.
Add last 2 ingredients before time to eat.

Where Are We?

Two **blondes** were driving through Louisiana. As they approached the town of Lafayette, they started arguing about the pronunciation of the name. They continued to argue until they stopped for lunch. As they stood at the counter, one **blonde** asked the manager, "Before we order, can you please settle an argument for us? Would you pronounce the name of where we are?" The manager leaned over the counter and said, "BURRRRRRRRR-GERRRRRRRR-KIIIIIIING."

In Louisiana
(Cajun Food)

Louisiana Roast Beef
"If You Aren't Slitting, You Aren't Fitting"

1	**bell pepper, finely chopped**
4	**ribs of celery, finely chopped**
1	**onion, finely chopped**
1/2	**stick margarine, melted**
1	**teaspoon each salt & pepper**
1/2	**teaspoon dry mustard**
1/2	**teaspoon cayenne pepper**
3/4	**teaspoon minced garlic**
1	**4 pound boneless sirloin roast**

Combine 1st 8 ingredients together.
Make 10 deep slits in meat, to form a pocket
Fill pockets with vegetable mixture
Bake at 300 degrees **uncovered** for 3 hours.
Pour drippings from pan on roast.

Run, Freddie, Run!

Freddie, a **blonde**, was driving his pickumup truck down the levee pretty fast one day. A Louisiana State Trooper spotted Freddie, and took off after him, but Freddie just kept going faster and faster. The tropper turned his lights and siren on, but Freddie just kept going. After about twenty miles, Freddie ran out of gas, and had to stop. The tropper jumped out of his car yelling at Freddie, "Why didn't you stop? I know you saw me!" Freddie replied, "Well, officer, I'm truly sorry for dat. But you see, a few years ago my wife, Neppie, she rund off wid a state trooper, and when I saw you, I thought you was him tryin' to bring her back. So I was tryin' to get away fast."

Chicken Creole
"Cajun Spatchcock"

4	chicken breasts, skinless, boneless, cut in 1 inch strips
1/2	stick margarine
1	(16 ounce) can diced tomatoes
1	cup chili sauce
1	bell pepper, chopped
1	onion, chopped
1	teaspoon basil
1/4	teaspoon crushed red pepper
1	(12 ounce) penne pasta, cooked according to directions

Sauté 1st 2 ingredients together in skillet for 10 minutes
Reduce heat. **Add** next 6 ingredients. **Bring** to a boil.
Reduce heat. **Simmer** covered for 10 minutes.
Serve over hot pasta.

NO SWIMMING!!!

A **blonde** lady camper in Lafayette decided to take a dip in the lake with her dog despite signs saying: "No Swimming – Alligators."

The **blonde** swam to an island about 75 yards from the shore, then saw some alligators and refused to swim back.

"Didn't you see the signs?" asked a worker who retrieved her in a canoe.

"Sure," she said, "But I didn't think it applied to me."

Crawfish Pie
"Mud Bug or Jayne Bug"

1	stick margarine
1	bell pepper, finely chopped
3	ribs of celery, finely chopped
1	onion, finely chopped
1	(8 ounce) can tomato sauce
1	pound crawfish tailmeat
$1/2$	cup Italian breadcrumbs
	Salt & pepper to taste
1	egg, beaten

Sauté 1st 4 ingredients together until tender.
Add next 2 ingredients. **Simmer** for 10 minutes.
Turn off heat. **Add** last 3 ingredients. **Mix** well.
Pour into pam-sprayed pie dish.
Bake at 350 degrees for 15-20 minutes.

His Last Breath

Boudreaux was on his last dying breath. He was upstairs in the waterbed and was about to slip out of this world when he smelled it. The most wonderful smell. Brownies, baking in the oven downstairs.

He struggled out of the waterbed. He could not stand up, so he crawled over the stairway and rolled down the stairs. He crawled into the kitchen and pulled himself up to the counter where the brownies were cooling on the rack. He took one and put it to his month. Awe! That wonderful smell, that wonderful taste.

Anne, a **blonde**, walked up behind him and said, "Shame on you Boudreaux. Those brownies are for after the funeral."

Oyster-Shrimp Pasta
"Limpy at the Boat House"

1	onion, finely chopped
3	ribs of celery, finely chopped
1	pound shrimp, peeled
1	stick margarine
1	pound oysters, drained, quartered
1	pint half-&-half
2	Tablespoons creole seasoning
$^1/_2$	teaspoon Blonde Lemon-Pepper
12	ounces pasta, cooked according to directions

Sauté 1st 4 ingredients until tender.
Add next 4 ingredients. **Cook** for 5 minutes over medium heat.
Add the pasta and **toss** well. **Let set** for 10 minutes.

Boat For Sale?

While Bill was fishing he died. His wife, Anne, a **blonde**, sent his obituary in to the newspaper. It said: *Bill died yesterday while fishing.* The newspaper people called her and said you can put a little more in the paper. You have 10 lines. So the next day the obituary appeared in the paper: *Bill died while fishing yesterday. Boat For Sale.*

Sweet Cajun Shrimp & Rice
"Hot & Sweet Tiger"

1   cup ketchup
1   Tablespoon brown sugar
1   Tablespoon honey
1   teaspoon salt
1   teaspoon cayenne pepper
2   Tablespoons balsamic vinegar
2   teaspoons hot sauce
1   pound shrimp, peeled
4   cups rice, cooked

Combine 1st 7 ingredients in sauce pan.
Heat thoroughly. **Add** shrimp, **cook** for 5-10 minutes.
Serve over rice.

Come Clean!

A **blonde** Cajun went to a store looking for detergent. The store clerk asked if he had a lot of clothing to wash. The **blonde** Cajun said, "No, I need to wash my dog." The clerk warned him: "It is strong. It will make the dog sick or even kill your dog." The **blonde** Cajun kept it anyway and went to pay for it. One week later the **blonde** Cajun went back to buy beer. When he went to pay for it the clerk ask "How is your dog?" The **blonde** Cajun said that the dog died. The clerk didn't want to be mean and say, "I told you so," so he just asked what did it. The **blonde** Cajun said, "I think it was the spin cycle."

Louisiana Jambalaya
"Balayez"

2	pounds smoked link sausage, sliced thin
1	onion, finely chopped
5	Tablespoons dried parsley
2	Tablespoons minced garlic
1/4	teaspoon ground thyme
2	(8 ounce) cans tomato sauce
2	cans water, use tomato sauce cans
2	pounds shrimp, peeled
4	cups cooked rice

Brown sausage and **drain** fat off.
Add next 6 ingredients in saucepan.
Bring to a boil. **Reduce** heat.
Cook for 45 minutes. **Add** shrimp.
Cook 5-10 minutes.
Serve over rice.

Comfortable Blonde

A **blonde** and a brunette are running a ranch in Louisiana. The brunette takes her life savings of $600.00 and goes to Texas to buy a bull. She eventually meets with an old cowboy that will sell her a bull for $599.00.

She buys the bull and goes to the telegram office and asks to send a telegram to her friend that says, "Have found the stud bull for our ranch, bring the trailer." The man tells her each word costs 75 cents. She thinks about it and says, "I'd like to send one word please." "And what word would that be," inquires the man. "Comfortable," replies the brunette. " You see my friend is a **blonde** and she reads real slow. When she gets this she will read COM FOR THE BULL."

Chocolate Praline Bundt Cake
"Pure D Goode"

1	stick margarine
2	cups whipping cream
1	cup brown sugar
1	cup pecans, chopped
1	box Devil's Food cake mix
1¼	cups water
⅓	cup oil
½	teaspoon vanilla
3	eggs, beaten

Combine 1st 3 ingredients together.
Cook over low heat, until margarine melts.
Pour into pam-sprayed bundt pan.
Sprinkle evenly with pecans.
Mix next 5 ingredients together.
Spoon over pecan mixture.
Bake at 325 degrees for 35-45 minutes. **Cool**.

Thought To Ponder

Confucious say: "**Blonde** who fly upside down have crack up."

With Meats

(Beef/Chicken/Pork/Seafood)

With Meats
(Beef/Chicken/Pork/Seafood)

One That Got Away

Once a **blonde** decided to go ice fishing. She grabbed all her equipment and put on her fishing outfit. She walked out onto the icy surface and found a good spot. She took a knife and made a large circle in the ice with it.

"NO! Not there! You will find no fish!" a booming voice announced out of nowhere. So the **blonde** moved a few feet away and made another circle. "NO!! Not there either!!" The voice boomed again. The **blonde** moved a third time, making another circle on the ice.

"I said, NO!! There is no fish there!!" The voice boomed again.

"Is that you, God?" The **blonde** called out.

"NO!!" The voice boomed. "It's the manager of the ice rink!!"

Beef Casserole with Potatoes
"Jake Me To Your Leader"

1¹/₂	**pounds ground beef**
¹/₂	**onion, chopped**
3	**potatoes, peeled, sliced**
2	**carrots, sliced**
1	**can cream of mushroom soup**
1	**(8 ounce) shredded cheddar cheese**

Brown 1st 2 ingredients until onions are tender. **Drain**.
Put in pam-sprayed 9x13 baking dish.
Layer next 3 ingredients in order given.
Bake at 350 degrees for 45-55 minutes.
Sprinkle with cheese. **Bake** until cheese melts.

Quick Beef Burgundy
"Deep Red Drunk"

2¹/₂	**pounds round steak**
1	**can golden mushroom soup**
1	**package dried onion soup mix**
1	**(4 ounce) can pieces & stem mushrooms**
1	**cup burgundy wine**
1	**(12 ounce) package wide egg noodles, cooked**

Cut beef in bite size pieces.
Place in pam-sprayed 9x13 baking dish.
Mix next 4 ingredients together.
Pour over beef.
Bake at 300 degrees **covered** for 3 hours, **don't** open door.
Serve over noodles.

Marinated Eye of the Round
"Marinating In The Sea Of Love"

1   **3 pound eye of round roast**

Marinade:
- **$^1/_4$**   **cup vegetable oil**
- **2**   **Tablespoons Blonde Lemon Pepper**
- **$^1/_2$**   **cup red wine vinegar**
- **$^1/_2$**   **cup lemon juice**
- **$^1/_2$**   **cup soy sauce**
- **$^1/_2$**   **cup Worcestershire sauce**
- **1**   **teaspoon Blonde All-Purpose Seasoning**
- **1**   **teaspoon salt**

Combine all marinade ingredients together.
Marinate roast in sauce overnight.
Place roast and marinade in pam-sprayed dish.
Bake at 300 degrees **uncovered** for 3 hours.
Refrigerate overnight. **Slice** thin.
Serve with heated marinade.

Q: Why did the platinum blonde go to the jewelry store?
A: To get her hair checked for value.

Chicken Cordon Bleu
"He's Chicken & Blue"

1	egg, beaten
1½	cups milk, divided
4	chicken breasts, boneless, skinless, cubed
1	cup bread crumbs
¼	cup oil
1	cup Swiss cheese, cubed
1	cup ham, diced
1	can cream of chicken soup
	Salt & pepper to taste

Combine egg & ½ cup milk. **Coat** chicken cubes.
Dip coated chicken in bread crumbs. **Brown** in oil.
Place chicken in pam-sprayed 9x13 baking dish.
Sprinkle cheese & ham over chicken.
Mix soup with 1 cup of milk and salt & pepper.
Pour over mixture.
Bake at 350 degrees for 30-45 minutes.

Paper Or Plastic?

A **blonde** was at the checkout line in the grocery store when the grocery bagger courteously asked the **blonde** woman, "Paper or plastic?" "It doesn't matter," she replied, "I'm bi-sacksual."

Chicken Medley
"Name That Chicken"

1 (16 ounce) frozen broccoli cuts, thawed, drained
1 (16 ounce) shredded cheddar cheese, divided
1/2 cup onion, chopped
4 chicken breasts, cooked, chopped
1 bell pepper, chopped
1/2 cup Bisquick
1 cup milk
2 eggs, beaten
1/2 cup sour cream

Layer first 5 ingredients, **using** 1 cup cheese, in pam-sprayed 9x13 baking dish.
Beat last 4 ingredients together.
Pour over mixture.
Bake at 400 degrees **uncovered** for 35 minutes.
Sprinkle remaining cheese on top.
Bake 5 more minutes.

Blonde Superstition

Two **blonde** robbers were robbing a hotel. The first one said, "I hear sirens. Jump!"

The second one said, "But we're on the 13th floor!"

The first one screamed back, "This is no time to be superstitious."

Almond Chicken
"He's All Man & He's Chicken"

1/2	onion, chopped
4	Tablespoons margarine
6	Tablespoons flour
1	can cream of chicken soup
2	cups milk
4	chicken breasts, cooked, chopped
1	(5 ounce) blanched slivered almonds
1	cup rice, cooked
1	(8 ounce) jar sliced mushrooms

Sauté 1st 2 ingredients. **Blend** in flour.
Slowly add next 2 ingredients.
Stir constantly until thick.
Combine next 5 ingredients.
Pour into pam-sprayed 9x13 baking dish.
Bake at 325 degrees **covered** for 20 minutes.
Uncover. **Bake** for 25 more minutes

Q: Why did the blonde bake a chicken for 3 and a half days?
A: It said cook it for half an hour per pound, and she weighed 125 pounds!

Honey Pork Loin
"Honey! Pork You"

1	**2-3 pound boneless pork loin**
1/4	**cup honey**
2	**Tablespoons Dijon mustard**
2	**Tablespoons pepper**
1/2	**teaspoon thyme**
1/2	**teaspoon salt**

Place pork in pam-sprayed 9x13 baking dish.
Combine next 5 ingredients.
Pour half of mixture over pork.
Bake at 325 degrees for 35 minutes.
Pour remaining mixture over pork and **bake** 35 more minutes.
Let stand 10 minutes before slicing.

Ham and Swiss Pie
"Swiss City Ham"

2	**cups ham, cooked, cubed**
1	**(8 ounce) shredded Swiss cheese**
2	**green onions, chopped**
4	**eggs, beaten**
2	**cups milk**
1	**cup Bisquick**

Layer 1st 3 ingredients in pam-sprayed 9x13 dish.
Beat last 3 ingredients together.
Pour into dish. **Bake** at 400 degrees for 30-40 minutes.

Ham Casserole
"Moore Ham & Nuts"

2	cans cream of chicken soup
4	ribs of celery, chopped
4	teaspoons minced onion
1	cup almonds, chopped
2	Tablespoons lemon juice
1¹/₂	cups mayonnaise
2	cups potato chips, crushed
2	cups cooked ham, chopped
6	hard boiled eggs, chopped

Mix 1st 7 ingredients together.
Put half of mixture in pam-sprayed 9x13 baking dish.
Cover with 3 eggs and 1 cup ham.
Layer again with mixture, eggs and ham.
Bake at 300 degrees for 30 minutes.

A Blonde In The Library!!

A **blonde** went in the library and walked up to the librarian behind the desk and said, "I would like a cheeseburger."

The librarian replied, "Shh! This a library!" the **blonde** blushed. "Oh! Sorry." Then she whispered, "I would like a cheeseburger."

Creole Catfish
"Jayne Bugs Cajun"

2	Tablespoons Creole seasoning, divided
2	cups heavy cream
2	Tablespoons Dijon mustard
8	catfish filets
1¹/₂	cups flour
1	cup canola oil

Blend 1 Tablespoon Creole & next 2 ingredients.
Pour over filets in a shallow dish.
Refrigerate for 30 minutes.
Mix flour and rest of Creole seasoning.
Dip filets in flour mixture until coated.
Sauté in hot oil 2 filets at a time for 3 minutes a side.

The Quarterback

A guy took his **blonde** girlfriend to her first football game. Afterward he asked her how she liked the game.

"I liked it, but I couldn't understand why they were killing each other for 25 cents," she said.

"What do you mean?"

"Well, everyone kept yelling, "Get the quarter back!"

Shrimp & Asparagus Casserole
"Oh Spare Us The Whine"

2	(12 ounce) cans asparagus, drained
1	(8 ounce) shredded cheddar cheese
1	cup Parmesan cheese
1	pound shrimp, cooked, peeled
2	eggs, beaten
1	cup white wine
1	Tablespoon Worcestershire
1	Tablespoon hot sauce
	Bread crumbs

Place asparagus in pam-sprayed 9x13 baking dish.
Sprinkle half the cheeses over asparagus.
Layer shrimp, then the remaining half of the cheeses.
Mix next 4 ingredients together.
Pour over shrimp and **sprinkle** with bread crumbs.
Bake at 350 degrees for 1 hour.

A Blonde Fire!!!

Two **blondes** realized that their apartment was on fire and went out onto the balcony.

"Help, Help!" yells one of the **blondes**.

"Help us, Help us!" yells the other.

"Maybe it would help if we yelled together," said the first **blonde**.

"Good idea," said the other.

"Together, together!"

Seafood Pasta Casserole
"Limpy Shrimpy Wimpy"

1	can cream of shrimp soup
2/3	cup milk
1	(16 ounce) shredded cheddar cheese
1/2	cup mayonnaise
1	(16 ounce) uncooked noodles, crushed
1/2	pound fresh shrimp or 4.5 ounce can
1/2	pound fresh crab meat or 6 ounce can
1	(8 ounce) can sliced water chestnuts, drained
	Salt & pepper to taste

Mix all ingredients together.
Pour in a pam-sprayed 2 quart casserole dish.
Bake at 325 **covered** for 20-30 minutes.
Uncover. **Bake** 10-20 more minutes.

Q: What did the blonde do when she heard that 90% of accidents occur around the home?
A: She moved.

On New Year's Day

On New Year's Day

What Is Her Real Color?

There was this typical peroxide **blonde**. She was really tired of being made fun of and being called a ditz, so she decided to get a makeover. She went to a salon and had her hair done so that she was, once again, a brunette. Now that she was a brunette, she decided she would take a drive in the country. So she hopped into her convertible and started driving. She saw a farmer and a flock of sheep and thought, "Oh! Those sheep are so adorable!" She got out and walked over to the farmer and said, "If I can guess how many sheep you have, can I take one home?" The farmer, looking skeptical, said she could. So the **blonde** looked at the flock and said, "157." The farmer was amazed because she was right. She picked one out and was getting in her car when the farmer walked up to her and said, "If I can guess the real color of your hair, can I have my dog back?"

Champagne Mimosa
"Fermented Evening"

1   cup strawberry daiquiri mix
1   (6 ounce) can frozen orange juice, thawed
$^1/_3$ cup grapefruit juice
$^3/_4$ cup water
$^1/_3$ cup frozen limeade, thawed
$^1/_3$ cup frozen lemonade, thawed
$^1/_3$ cup frozen pink lemonade, thawed
      Chilled champagne
      Orange slices

Mix 1st 7 ingredients together in a pitcher.
Chill until serving.
Pour over ice in glasses, **filling** half full.
Fill with champagne. **Garnish** with orange slices.

Champagne Cheese Spread
"Vin Mousseux Spread"

1   (8 ounce) gorgonzola cheese, softened
1   stick margarine, softened
$^3/_4$ cup champagne
      Cayenne pepper to taste
      Salt to taste
      Cavendar's Greek seasoning to taste

Combine all ingredients together.
Serve with crackers.

Hot Turnip Green Dip
"Brassica Rapa Root"

$^1/_2$ cup onion, finely chopped
2   ribs of celery, finely chopped
2   Tablespoons margarine
1   (4 ounce) can mushrooms, drained
1   (10 ounce) frozen chopped turnip greens
1   can cream of mushroom soup
1   (6 ounce) roll garlic cheese
1   teaspoon Worcestershire
5   drops hot pepper sauce

Sauté 1st 3 ingredients together until tender.
Stir in mushrooms. **Set** aside.
Cook greens according to package directions & **drain**.
Combine all ingredients together in top of double boiler.
Serve hot with corn chips.

Blue Cheese Cole Slaw
"Shred Her Blues"

2   (4 ounce) packages shredded carrots
3   (16 ounce) packages prepared cole slaw
1   (15 ounce) jar Marzetti slaw dressing
1   pound bacon, cooked crisp, crumbled
3   (4 ounce) packages crumbled blue cheese
   Salt & pepper to taste

Mix all ingredients together in large bowl.
Toss. **Chill**.

Beefy Cabbage Soup
"He Pilfered The Night Away"

1	pound ground beef, browned, drained
1	onion, chopped
1	bell pepper, chopped
3	cups water
1	(16 ounce) bag prepared cole slaw
1	(14.5 ounce) can diced tomatoes
1	teaspoon salt
2	(16 ounce) cans kidney beans
1	Tablespoon chili powder

Combine first 5 ingredients together in stock pot.
Cover and **cook** for 20 minutes.
Combine remaining ingredients.
Cover and **cook** until boiling.
Reduce heat and **simmer** for 1 hour.

Locked Her Keys In The Car!

A **blonde** is driving down the road. She notices that she is low on gas, so she stops at the gas station. While pumping her gas, she notices that she had locked the keys in the car. So when she goes inside to pay, the **blonde** asks the attendant for a coat hanger so she can attempt to open the door herself.

She goes outside and begins to jimmy the lock. Ten minutes later, the attendant goes outside to see how the **blonde** is faring. The **blonde** outside of the car is moving the hanger around and around.

Meanwhile, the **blonde** inside of the car is saying. "A little more to the left. A little more to the right..."

Ham Cabbage Chowder
"He's Heavy & Rough"

2	ribs of celery, chopped
1	small onion, chopped
3	Tablespoons margarine
1	(16 ounce) bag prepared cole slaw
3	cups cooked ham, diced
2	(16 ounce) cans Mexican-style stewed tomatoes
1	(15 ounce) can whole-kernel corn
1	(14.5 ounce) can chicken broth
1	cup water

Sauté 1st 3 ingredients together until tender.
Add all ingredients in large pot.
Bring to a boil. **Reduce** heat.
Cover. **Simmer** for 1 hour.

Q: Why don't blondes double recipes?
A: The oven doesn't go to 700 degrees.

Jalapeño
Black-Eyed Pea Salad
"Hot Edible Black Spot"

2	(16 ounce) cans jalapeño black-eyed peas
1	ripe avocado, peeled, chopped
1/2	red onion, chopped
3	ribs of celery, chopped
1	bell pepper, chopped

Mix all ingredients together.

Dressing:

1/3	cup oil
1/3	cup balsamic vinegar
3	Tablespoons sugar
1/4	teaspoon garlic powder

Mix all dressing ingredients together.
Combine salad & dressing. **Toss**. **Chill**.

Q: What do you call a basement full of blondes?
A: A whine cellar.

Marinated Black-Eyed Pea Toss
"Borrow Sorrow Morrow"

2	(15 ounce) cans black-eyed peas, drained
1	small red onion, chopped
1	bell pepper, chopped
$1/4$	cup balsamic vinegar
$1/4$	cup sugar
$1/4$	cup oil
	Salt to taste
	Pepper to taste
	Dash of hot sauce

Combine all ingredients together. **Toss** lightly.
Cover & **refrigerate** at least 12 hours.

Q: What do UFO's and smart blondes have in common?
A: You hear about them all the time, but you never see one.

Cheesy Cabbage
"Who's Cheesy Kale Or Savell?"

2   (16 ounce) bags prepared cole slaw
1   (16 ounce) small-curd cottage cheese
1   (16 ounce) shredded cheddar cheese
1   cup water
4   eggs, beaten
3   Tablespoons flour
1/2   stick margarine, melted
1/4   teaspoon garlic salt
1/4   teaspoon Blonde Lemon-Pepper

Mix all ingredients together.
Put in pam-sprayed 2 quart baking dish.
Bake at 350 degrees for 1 hour.

Q: What's five miles long and has an IQ of forty?
A: A **blonde** parade.

New Year's Hush Puppy
"Did You Get Fried? Hush!"

1	small onion, finely chopped
3	Tablespoons olive oil
2	(15 ounce) cans black-eyed peas, drained
1	(8 ounce) cream cheese, softened
1	egg, beaten
2	teaspoons hot sauce
$1/2$	teaspoon salt
1	(8 ounce) package hush puppy mix
	Blonde Pepper Jelly

Sauté 1st 2 ingredients together until tender.
Combine next 5 ingredients in food processor.
Add hush puppy mix.
Combine all ingredients together, except pepper jelly.
Use 2 tablespoons of mixture to make small patties.
Place on a baking sheet covered with wax paper.
Chill for 1 hour.
Place patties in skillet with heated olive oil.
Sauté for four minutes on each side or until crisp.
Drain on paper towels.
Garnish with pepper jelly.

Q: Why should blondes not be given coffee breaks?
A: Because it take's too long to retrain them.

Sweet and Sour Pork
"Did You Pork Her?"

4   boneless pork chops, browned, cubed
1   green bell pepper, cut into strips
1   red bell pepper, cut into strips
1   onion, chopped
1   (16 ounce) can pineapple chunks, with juice
1   (8 ounce) bottle Catalina French salad dressing
1   package dry onion soup mix
1   Tablespoon soy sauce
2   cups rice, cooked

Layer 1st 4 ingredients in pam-sprayed 9x13 dish.
Mix next 4 ingredients together.
Pour over layered ingredients.
Bake at 350 degrees for 1 hour.
Serve over rice.

Q: How do four blondes carpool to work?
A: They all meet at work at 7:45.

Brown Sugar Rum Cake
"She Was A Fermented Sugar"

3	sticks margarine, melted
1	(16 ounce) box brown sugar
1	cup sugar
5	eggs, beaten
$3/4$	cup milk
$1/4$	cup rum
2	teaspoons vanilla
3	cups self-rising flour
1	cup pecans, chopped

Combine all ingredients together.
Pour in pam-sprayed bundt pan.
Bake at 325 degrees for 1 hour & 10 minutes.

A Blonde Selling Her Car????

A **blonde** wanted to sell her old car, but nobody wanted to buy a car with 250,000 miles on it. So, she tells her brunette girlfriend at the salon about her problem, and the brunette suggests she take the car to a mechanic friend of hers, who will turn the meter back by 200,000 miles.

The **blonde** thinks this is a great suggestion and does so.

About a month later, the brunette sees her **blonde** girlfriend in a store and says, "Did you ever sell your car?"

"No," says the **blonde**. "Why should I? It only has 50,000 miles on it."

Over & Over & Over

(Leftovers)

Over & Over & Over
(Leftovers)

The Blonde & The Ventriloquist

A young ventriloquist was touring the nightclubs and one night he was doing a show in a small club in Alabama. With his dummy on his knee, he's going through his usual dumb **blonde** jokes when a **blonde** woman in the 4th row stands on her chair. "I've heard enough of your stupid **blonde** jokes. What does the color of a person's hair have to do with her worth as a human being? It's guys like you who keep women like me from being respected at work and in the community and from reaching our full potential as a person...because you and your kind continue to perpetuate discrimination against, not only **blondes**, but women in general . . and all in the name of humor!"

The ventriloquist was extremely embarrassed and begins to apologize, when the **blonde** yells, "You stay out of this, mister! I'm talking to that little smart mouth on your knee."

Over & Over & Over
(Leftovers)

Leftover Coffee
"Is It Black Joe?"

2	pound boneless sirloin roast, cut in half
2	teaspoons oil
1	(8 ounce) sliced fresh mushrooms
1¹/₂	cups brewed coffee
1	teaspoon liquid smoke
¹/₂	teaspoon chili powder
	Salt & pepper to taste
¹/₄	cup cornstarch
¹/₃	cup water

Brown roast in oil on medium high heat.
Place roast in crock pot.
Sauté next 5 ingredients in same skillet.
Pour over roast.
Cook for 8-10 hours on medium setting.
Remove roast and **keep** warm.
Pour cooking juices into a 2-cup measuring cup.
Skim Fat.
Combine last 2 ingredients.
Stir in 2 cups cooked juices.
Bring to a boil.
Cook until sauce is thick.
Serve over sliced beef.

Q: Why do blondes wear ponytails?
A: To hide the valve stem!

Leftover Chicken
"A Leftover Chick"

3	cups leftover cooked chicken, chopped
1	bell pepper, chopped
1	(4 ounce) can mushrooms
$^1/_2$	teaspoon poultry seasoning
2	cans cream of mushroom soup
1	cup milk
	Salt & pepper to taste
1	(2 ounce) jar sliced pimientos, drained
1	(5 ounce) can chow mein noodles

Combine 1st 4 ingredients together.
Pour into pam-sprayed 9x13 baking dish.
Blend next 4 ingredients together.
Pour over chicken mixture.
Sprinkle chow mein noodles over top.
Bake at 350 degrees for 30-35 minutes.

Q: How can you tell if a blonde writes mysteries?
A: She has a checkbook.

Over & Over & Over
(Leftovers)

Leftover Crawfish
"Corny Crawfish"

1   (8 ounce) cream cheese
1   stick margarine
4   green onions, chopped
2   cans cream of potato soup
1   (15 ounce) can whole-kernel corn
1   (15 ounce) can cream-style corn
2   cups milk
1   Tablespoon cajun seasoning
3   cups cooked crawfish tails

Melt slowly 1st 2 ingredients in pot.
Add onions and **simmer** for 10-15 minutes.
Stir in soup and corns, then **simmer** for 15 minutes.
Add milk **stirring** constantly.
Before ready to serve **add** last 2 ingredients.

Blonde Roots

"**Blondes** have more fun," don't they? They must. How many brunettes do you see walking down the street with **blonde** roots?"

Over & Over & Over
(Leftovers)

Leftover Ham
"Where Did This Stem From?"

1 onion, finely chopped
2 Tablespoons margarine
6 cups cooked ham, chopped
1 (8 ounce) can mushroom stems & pieces
2 cans cream of mushroom soup
1 (8 ounce) sour cream

Sauté 1st 2 ingredients together.
Add next 3 ingredients.
Mix well.
Simmer for 30 minutes.
Add sour cream. **Cook** 15 minutes.
Serve over noodles or rice.

Leftover Pork
"A Hot Blonde Pick"

3 cups cooked pork, shredded
1 (8 ounce) shredded cheddar cheese
1 (4 ounce) can green chilies
1 teaspoon minced onion
1/4 teaspoon Blonde Lemon-Pepper
12 flour tortillas

Mix 1st 5 ingredients together. **Heat** thoroughly.
Place a large tablespoon of pork mixture in tortilla.
Roll up & **secure** with a toothpick.

162

Leftover Turkey, Ham, & Cranberry Sauce
"DeTox Me...Turkey!"

1	cup sugar
1	cup water
1	(16 ounce) can whole cranberry sauce
1/4	cup ketchup
1	Tablespoon lemon juice
4	cups cooked turkey & ham, cubed

Combine first 2 ingredients.
Heat to a boiling point for 5 minutes.
Add cranberry sauce. **Cook** for 5 minutes.
Stir in ketchup & lemon juice.
Place turkey & ham in sauce.
Cook on low for 10 minutes.

Q: Why do blondes wear their hair up?
A: To catch everything that goes over their heads.

Over & Over & Over
(Leftovers)

Leftover Baked Potatoes
"Rich & Owening"

1	stick margarine
$2/3$	cup self-rising flour
7	cups milk
4	baked potatoes, peeled, cubed
12	strips of bacon, cooked, crumbled
1	(8 ounce) shredded cheddar cheese
1	(8 ounce) sour cream
	Salt to taste
	Pepper to taste

Combine 1st 2 ingredients in large saucepan.
Heat & **stir** until smooth.
Add milk, **stirring** constantly until thickened.
Add potatoes. **Bring** to a boil.
Reduce heat. **Simmer** for 10 minutes.
Add remaining ingredients. **Stir** until cheese melts.

Q: What do you call a blonde in a tree with a brief case?
A: Branch Manager.

Over & Over & Over
(Leftovers)

Leftover Roast Beef
"Mary Kate Or Ashley?"

2	cups cooked roast beef, chopped
2	cups water
2	beef bouillon cubes
$^1/_2$	onion, chopped
1	potato, peeled, chopped
1	teaspoon flour

Simmer 1st 5 ingredients together for 20-25 minutes.
Add flour to thicken.

Leftover Shrimp
"He's A Cooked Runt"

1	stick margarine
2	teaspoons minced garlic
3	green onions, chopped
3	cans cream of potato soup
3	(8 ounce) cream cheese, cut into small cubes
1	pound cooked shrimp, cut into 3 pieces
6	soup cans of milk
1	teaspoon cayenne pepper
	Salt & pepper to taste

Sauté 1st 3 ingredients in stock pot.
Add remaining ingredients. **Simmer** for 30 minutes.

Leftover Spaghetti Sauce
"Layer Me Again"

2	cups spaghetti sauce
1	(7 ounce) spaghetti noodles
2	eggs, beaten
1/2	cup parmesan cheese
1	(8 ounce) cottage cheese
1	(8 ounce) shredded mozzarella cheese

Warm spaghetti sauce.
Cook noodles according to package & **drain**.
Combine noodles with next 2 ingredients.
Pour into pam-sprayed pie plate.
Spoon cottage cheese over noodles.
Top with spaghetti sauce.
Bake at 350 degrees for 20 minutes.
Place cheese on top. **Bake** until cheese melts.

Q: What's the difference between a blonde and a computer?
A: You only have to punch information into a computer once.

Over & Over & Over
(Leftovers)

Leftover Turkey Divine
"Head Forming Turkey"

$1/2$	cup olive oil, divided
$1/3$	cup walnuts, chopped
2	bags Romaine lettuce
2	cups cooked turkey, diced
$1/2$	cup Swiss cheese, cubed
2	peaches, peeled, diced

Heat $1/4$ cup oil & walnuts for 6-8 minutes. **Set** aside.
Mix next 4 ingredients together in large bowl.
Add walnuts.

Dressing:

3	Tablespoons raspberry vinegar
$1/2$	teaspoon Dijon mustard
$1/3$	cup olive oil

Whisk all dressing ingredients together.
Pour over lettuce mixture.

Q: What does a blonde say when you ask her if her blinker is working?
A: Yes. No. Yes. No. Yes. No. Yes. No. Yes. No.

Over & Over & Over
(Leftovers)

Leftover Turkey
"The Second Time Was A Real Turkey"

1	(8 ounce) shredded cheddar cheese
1	Tablespoon flour
1	(2.25 ounce) slivered almonds
3	cups cooked turkey, chopped
2	ribs of celery, chopped
1	Tablespoon lemon juice
1	cup mayonnaise
$^1/_2$	teaspoon poultry seasoning
2	pie crusts (refrigerated section)

Mix 1st 8 ingredients together.
Place pie crust in pie pan.
Pour mixture in pie crust.
Cover with 2nd pie crust.
Bake at 400 degrees for 30-35 minutes.

Q: What happened to the blonde tap dancer?
A: She slipped off and fell down the drain.

With Pasta

With Pasta

A Blonde Lottery Ticket

A **blonde** woman named Debbie finds herself in trouble. Her business has gone bust and she's in serious financial straits. She's so desperate that she decides to ask God for help. She begins to pray ... "God, please help me. I've lost my business and if I don't get some money, I'm going to lose my house. Please let me win the lottery." Lottery night comes and she does not win. Debbie prays again, but still she doesn't win. Once again, she prays ... "God, why have you forsaken me? I've lost my business, my house, and my car. My children are starving. I don't often ask for help, and I have always been a good servant to you. PLEASE just let me win the lottery this one time so I can get my life back in order." Suddenly, there is a blinding flash of light as the heavens open and Debbie is confronted by the voice of God himself ... "Debbie, work with me on this. Buy a ticket."

Lemon Spaghetti Salad
"A Little Stringy Gamboge"

²/₃	cup olive oil
²/₃	cup Parmesan cheese
¹/₂	cup lemon juice
2	Tablespoon Blonde Lemon-Pepper
1	(7 ounce) package spaghetti noodles
¹/₂	cup basil

Whisk 1st 4 ingredients together.
Bring a large pot of salted water to a boil.
Add spaghetti. **Cook** until tender.
Drain, reserving 1 cup of the spaghetti liquid.
Add spaghetti to lemon sauce and **toss**.
Add basil to spaghetti.
Toss the spaghetti with reserved liquid.

Strolling

One day, a **blonde** and her friend were walking through the park. Suddenly, the **blonde's** friend said, "Oh, look, a dead birdie!" The **blonde** looked up and said, "Where?"

Macaroni & Cheese Salad
"Yankee Doodle Dandy"

1	(7.25 ounce) box macaroni & cheese dinner
3	ribs of celery, chopped
1	bell pepper, chopped
1	(4 ounce) jar diced pimientos, drained
$^1/_2$	cup mayonnaise
1	Tablespoon balsamic vinegar

Cook macaroni and cheese according to package.
Add macaroni and cheese to remaining ingredients. **Chill**.

Spaghetti Salad
"Watch What You Wish For"

1	(8 ounce) bottle Italian dressing
1	package dry Italian dressing mix
$^1/_3$	bottle Salad Supreme seasoning
$^1/_2$	red onion, chopped
$^1/_2$	green pepper, chopped
1	(8 ounce) package vermicelli noodles, cooked

Mix 1st 5 ingredients together.
Toss in noodles.
Refrigerate overnight before serving.

With Pasta

Tortellini Salad
"Twisted & Stuffed"

2	(7 ounce) tortellini, cooked according to package
1	(10 ounce) bag frozen corn, cooked
$^1/_2$	red onion, chopped
1	bell pepper, chopped
$^1/_2$	cup parmesan cheese
1	(8 ounce) bottle oil & vinegar salad dressing

Combine all ingredients together.
Toss. **Refrigerate** overnight.

Vermicelli Toss
"It's A Toss Up"

1	(8 ounce) vermicelli, broken in half
1	Tablespoon margarine
1	(8 ounce) sour cream
1	(8 ounce) shredded sharp cheddar cheese
1	Tablespoon minced garlic
	Salt and pepper to taste

Cook vermicelli according to package, **drain**.
Add rest of ingredients & **return** to low heat.
Toss gently until cheese melts.

Broccoli-Pasta Soup
"Sprout It Out"

4   (14.5 ounce) cans chicken broth
1   (12 ounce) extra thin egg noodles
2   (10 ounce) frozen chopped broccoli
6   cups milk
1   pound Velveeta cheese, cubed
    Salt & pepper to taste

Bring chicken broth to a boil.
Add noodles. **Boil** for 4 minutes.
Add broccoli. **Boil** for 6 minutes.
Add last 4 ingredients, **stirring** until cheese melts.
Simmer for 45 minutes.

Beef Bow Tie Pasta
"Paste Me"

1   pound ground beef, browned, drained
2   tomatoes, chopped
1   (6 ounce) bow tie pasta, cooked
2   Tablespoons basil
3   Tablespoons grated parmesan cheese
    Salt & pepper to taste

Combine all ingredients together. **Chill**.

Chicken Macaroni Casserole
"I Elbowed That Chick"

1   (6 ounce) elbow macaroni, cooked
1   (8 ounce) shredded cheddar cheese
2   chicken breasts, cooked, diced
1   (8 ounce) can mushroom stems & pieces
1   can cream of mushroom soup
1   cup milk

Mix all ingredients together.
Pour into pam-sprayed 9x13 baking dish.
Bake at 350 degrees covered for 1 hour.

Chicken-Sloppy Joe Pasta
"That Chick Is Sloppy Joe!"

1   (12 ounce) rotini pasta, cooked according
       to directions.
3   chicken breasts, cooked, cut into bite-sized
       chunks
1   (12 ounce) can sloppy joe sauce
1   (8 ounce) shredded cheddar cheese
$^1/_2$ teaspoon salt
$^1/_2$ teaspoon pepper

Combine all ingredients together.
Pour into pam-sprayed 9x13 baking dish.
Bake at 325 degrees for 30-40 minutes.

Pepperoni Pasta Salad
"Spicy Phony"

1 (8 ounce) pasta, cooked according to directions
1 small bunch broccoli, cut into bite-size pieces
1 zucchini, sliced
1 bell pepper, chopped
1 (4 ounce) pepperoni, cubed
1 (8 ounce) mozzarella cheese, cubed
1 (6 ounce) jar artichoke hearts, cut in pieces
1 (8 ounce) bottle Italian dressing
  Salt & pepper to taste

Combine all ingredients together.
Cover & **chill** for 2 hours.

Right Side Up!

A **blonde** saw a "¿" on her computer screen and asked another **blonde**, "How do you do that?"
She responded … "Simple, turn the keyboard upside down!"

Sausage Rigatoni Pasta
"Grooved Tube"

1	pound Italian sausage, browned, drained
1	(12 ounce) frozen green peas
1^1/$_2$	cups heavy cream
4	Tablespoons margarine
1	(8 ounce) sour cream
2	Tablespoons grated parmesan cheese
^{1}/$_2$	teaspoon salt
^{1}/$_2$	teaspoon pepper
1	(12 ounce) rigatoni pasta, cooked according to directions

Simmer 1st 2 ingredients together for 5 minutes.
Add next 6 ingredients. **Simmer** for 10 minutes.
Add pasta. **Toss**.

It's Just Not Right!

A **blonde** woman competed with a brunette woman and a redheaded woman in the Breast Stroke division of an English Channel swim competition. The brunette came in first, and the redhead came in second.

The **blonde** woman finally reached the shore completely exhausted. After being revived with blankets and coffee the **blonde** remarked, "I don't want to complain, but I think those other two girls used their arms."

Shrimp-Cajun Salad
"Honey! Is that Wright?"

1	cup picante sauce
¹/₄	cup ketchup
¹/₄	teaspoon cajun seasoning
¹/₄	cup honey
1	red bell pepper, chopped
1	green bell pepper, chopped
¹/₂	pound shrimp, cooked, peeled
1	(12 ounce) spiral pasta, cooked
1	(4 ounce) can sliced black olives

Combine all ingredients together.
Toss. **Refrigerate**.

Blonde Windows

Last year a **blonde** replaced all her windows in her house. She kept receiving a bill. Frustrated, she called the bookkeeper and told her what the salesman said, "In one year the windows would pay for themselves."

A Quickie
(When You Are In A Hurry)

A Quickie
(When You Are In A Hurry)

Do It Yourself Blondes!

Two **blondes** living together decided to save some money by residing their house themselves. So they went out and bought all the equipment and started. One **blonde** handed the other a board which she then attached with some nails. However, while watching the one **blonde** nailing the boards in, the other noticed that when ever she pulled a nail out of the bag she would look at it and would sometimes throw one over her shoulder. She had to ask her friend what she was doing. Her friend said, "If I pull a nail out of the bag and it is facing me, I throw it away because it's defective." "It's not defective," said the other **blonde**, "It's for the other side of the house."

Red Pepper Dip
"Hot & Quick"

1	(8 ounce) cream cheese, softened
1	(8 ounce) sour cream
1	(8 ounce) shredded sharp cheddar cheese
$1/2$	(4 ounce) can chopped jalapeño peppers
1	red bell pepper, finely chopped
$1/2$	teaspoon ground cumin

Combine all ingredients together.
Refrigerate. **Serve** with crackers.

Swiss Cheese Dip
"Dot It With Joe"

8	pieces of bacon, fried, crumbled
$1^1/2$	cups shredded Swiss cheese
1	(8 ounce) cream cheese, softened
$1/2$	cup mayonnaise
3	green onions, chopped
$1/4$	cup sliced almonds

Combine 1st 5 ingredients together.
Put in pam-sprayed 9x9 baking dish.
Bake at 400 degrees for 20 minutes.
Sprinkle with almonds. **Bake** 5 more minutes.

A Quickie
(When You Are In A Hurry)

Crunchy Pea Salad
"Nutty Peas"

$1/3$ cup ranch dressing
$1/3$ cup mayonnaise
1   Tablespoon lemon juice
$1/4$ teaspoon celery seed
$1/4$ teaspoon salt
$1/4$ teaspoon pepper
1   (20 ounce) bag frozen peas, thawed
$1/2$ onion, finely chopped
1   cup salted peanuts

Mix 1st 8 ingredients together.
When ready to serve **add** peanuts.

Cheese Pasta Bake
"Paste His Noodle"

1   (16 ounce) noodles, cooked, drained
1   can cheddar cheese soup
1   (26 ounce) jar spaghetti sauce
1   teaspoon black pepper
1   (16 ounce) shredded mozzarella cheese, divided
1   teaspoon Italian seasoning

Combine all ingredients, except 1 cup of mozzarella.
Place in pam-sprayed 9x13 baking dish.
Bake at 400 degrees for 25 minutes.
Sprinkle with remaining cheese and **bake** for 5 more minutes.

Shoe Peg Corn Casserole
"Peg Was Pegged"

3   (12 ounce) cans shoe peg corn
2   ribs of celery, chopped
1   bell pepper, chopped
1   (8 ounce) shredded cheddar cheese
1   can cream of celery soup
1   (8 ounce) sour cream
1   can Rotel tomatoes
1   sleeve Ritz crackers, crumbled
1   stick margarine, melted

Mix 1st 7 ingredients together.
Place in pam-sprayed 9x13 baking dish.
Top with last 2 ingredients.
Bake at 350 degrees for 45 minutes.

A Shooting We Will Go!

I told my **blonde** girlfriend that I was going skeet shooting. She told me she didn't know how to cook them.

A Quickie
(When You Are In A Hurry)

Beef Salad
"Anne You Are Crushed?"

1	pound ground beef, cooked, drained
1	head of lettuce, chopped
1	red onion, chopped
1	tomato, chopped
1	(8 ounce) shredded cheddar cheese
1	(15 ounce) can ranch style beans
1	(5 ounce) catalina French dressing
1	(4 ounce) can chopped black olives
1	(13 ounce) bag Doritos chips, crushed

Combine 1st 8 ingredients together.
Add chips **when** ready to serve.

Chicken Asparagus Casserole
"That Chick Needs To Spare Us"

4	boneless, skinless chicken breasts
2	(12 ounce) cans asparagus, drained
2	cans cream of chicken soup
1	cup mayonnaise
1	(8 ounce) shredded cheddar cheese
1	cup bread crumbs

Boil chicken breasts for 20 minutes. **Drain** & **chop.**
Layer 1st 2 ingredients in pam-sprayed 2-quart dish.
Mix next 2 ingredients. **Pour** over chicken.
Top with last 2 ingredients.
Bake at 350 degrees for 20 minutes.

184

A Quickie
(When You Are In A Hurry)

Tuna Noodle Casserole
"A Warm Blooded Swimmer"

1   (6.5 ounce) can tuna fish
1   can cream of celery soup
1   cup milk
1   cup bread crumbs, divided
1   (8 ounce) egg noodles, cooked according to package
    Salt & pepper to taste

Mix 1st 3 ingredients together.
Add 3/4 cup crumbs & noodles. **Mix** well.
Pour in pam-sprayed 9x13 baking dish.
Sprinkle remaining crumbs, salt & pepper on top.
Bake at 375 degrees for 30 minutes.

Strawberry-Cream Cobbler
"Darryl, Are You A Strawberry?"

1   (quart) fresh strawberries, sliced
1   box yellow cake mix
1   box powdered sugar
1   stick margarine, melted
1   (8 ounce) cream cheese, softened
1   cup water

Mix all ingredients together thoroughly.
Pour into pam-sprayed 9x13 baking dish.
Bake at 350 degrees for 25-35 minutes.

Orange Cake
"Why Orange You A Peach?"

1 box orange cake mix
1/2 cup sour cream
2 eggs, beaten
1 (21 ounce) can peach pie filling

Combine all ingredients together.
Pour in pam-sprayed 9x13 baking pan.
Bake at 350 degrees for 20-30 minutes. **Cool**.

Topping:
1 small box instant vanilla pudding
1 (8 ounce) cream cheese, softened
1 (20 ounce) can crushed pineapple
1 (8 ounce) frozen whipped topping, thawed
1 teaspoon vanilla

Blend 1st 2 topping ingredients together.
Add next 3 ingredients.
Spread on cake.
Keep Refrigerated.

Not A Clue!

Postcard from a **blonde**: Having a wonderful time. Where am I?

No Bake Coconut Cream Pie
"He Has No Brains To Bake"

1	large box vanilla instant pudding
1¹/₂	cups milk
1¹/₂	cups flaked coconut
1	(8 ounce) frozen whipped topping, thawed
1	teaspoon vanilla
1	(9-inch) graham cracker crust

Combine 1ˢᵗ 5 ingredients together.
Pour into piecrust. **Chill**.

The One That Did Not Get Away!

One day a **blonde** was sitting in a bar trying to spear the olive in her drink with a toothpick, but the olive always eluded her. Finally, a guy sitting next to the **blonde** picked up a toothpick and said, "Here, this is how you do it," and neatly speared the olive. "Big deal," said the **blonde**, "I already had him so tired he couldn't get away."

A Quickie
(When You Are In A Hurry)

Peach Pie
"A Peach Fig Leaf"

1 (8 ounce) cream cheese, softened
3/4 cup powdered sugar
1/4 teaspoon almond extract
3/4 cup whipping cream, whipped
1 (16 ounce) can sliced peaches
1 (9-inch) graham cracker crust

Mix together 1st 3 ingredients. **Beat** until smooth
Fold in whipped cream and gently **stir** in peaches.
Pour filling into graham cracker crust.
Chill well before serving.

What Are The Odds?...A Real Fox!

The night before a **blonde** was supposed to appear in court he met his friend at a pub. Hearing the situation, his friend advised him to send the judge some fresh salmon beforehand. The next day the man tells his lawyer what his friend had told him, but the lawyer advised him not to do it as they could lose the case because they were already in a difficult position. They end up winning, to the amazement of he lawyer. "Did you send the judge the salmon?" asked the lawyer. "Well, yes," replied the **blonde,** "But I put the other side's name on it."

With Rice

With Rice

Tear Along The Dotted Line

There was a **blonde** driving down the center of the road at 100 mph. A police officer pulled her over to the side of the road. When she had stopped, the officer asked, "License and Registration, please." "It's okay, officer, I have a special license that allows me to do this," she said smiling. "That's impossible!" The officer replied, "I've never heard of such a license." The **blonde** reached into her purse and handed him her license. Astonished, the officer said, "Just as I suspected. This is an ordinary license, I see nothing here that would allow you special consideration." She pointed to the bottom of the license, "See! It says so right here: 'Tear Along The Dotted Line.' "

Shrimp & Rice Salad
"A Polished Runt"

1	head cauliflower, cut into bite-size pieces
1	cucumber, peeled, diced
1	pound baby shrimp, cooked, peeled
1	cup stuffed olives, chopped
4	cups rice, cooked
1	cup mayonnaise

Combine all ingredients together.
Refrigerate.

Tomato & Artichoke Rice Salad
"Are You Chokin' Me?"

2	(6 ounce) jars marinated artichoke hearts, quartered
2	Tablespoons lemon juice
$1/2$	teaspoon salt
$1/2$	teaspoon pepper
3	cups rice, cooked
3	large tomatoes, diced
$1/2$	red onion, finely chopped
1	(4 ounce) can sliced black olives
$1/4$	cup chopped parsley

Combine all ingredients together.
Refrigerate.

Chicken & Rice Soup
"A Shepard's Tune"

1	Tablespoon margarine
1/2	onion, finely chopped
1	(8 ounce) fresh sliced mushrooms
2	chicken breasts, cooked, chopped
1	Tablespoon Blonde All-Purpose Seasoning
3	(14.5 ounce) cans chicken broth
1	cup half & half
1	cup rice, cooked
1/4	cup cornstarch dissolved in 1/2 cup cold water

Sauté 1st 3 ingredients in skillet until tender.
Combine next 5 ingredients with 1st 3 in large saucepan.
Add cornstarch mixture. **Simmer** for 30 minutes.

Black-Eyed Pea Casserole
"Good Luck Tonite"

1	pound ground beef, cooked, drained
2	cups rice, cooked
2	(16 ounce) cans jalapeño black-eyed peas
1	(14.5 ounce) can diced tomatoes
1/2	onion, chopped
	Salt and pepper to taste

Combine all ingredients together.
Place in pam-sprayed 9x13 baking dish.
Bake at 350 degrees for 30 minutes.

Fried Rice
"Vahid Please!"

¹/₄	cup oil
4	cups rice, cooked
1	Tablespoon minced garlic
1	package dry onion soup mix
¹/₂	cup water
1	Tablespoon soy sauce
1	cup frozen peas and carrots, partially thawed
2	eggs, beaten
	Salt & pepper to taste

Heat oil. **Add** next 2 ingredients, **stirring** constantly.
Mix next 3 ingredients together then **pour** over rice.
Stir in peas and carrots.
Continue to stir 2-3 minutes.
Make a hole in center of rice, **stir** in eggs until cooked.
Toss all together before serving.

Rolex or Timex

A girl was visiting her **blonde** friend, who had acquired two new dogs, and asked her what their names were. The **blonde** responded by saying that one was named Rolex and one was named Timex. Her friend said, "Whoever heard of someone naming dogs like that?" "Hellooooo," answered the **blonde**. "They're watch dogs!"

193

Green Rice
"Whiz By Me"

1	**(16 ounce) bag frozen chopped broccoli**
1	**Tablespoon margarine**
$^1/_2$	**onion, finely chopped**
$^1/_2$	**cup light cream**
1	**can cream of chicken soup**
1	**cup rice, cooked**
$^1/_2$	**cup water**
1	**(8 ounce) can water chestnuts, chopped**
1	**(8 ounce) shredded cheddar cheese**

Cook broccoli according to directions.
Combine all ingredients together.
Pour into a pam-sprayed 9x13 baking dish.
Bake at 300 degrees for 30 minutes.

Rice Chop Suey
"She Is In Mixed Pieces"

1	**pound ground beef**
$^1/_2$	**onion, chopped**
1	**can cream of celery soup**
1	**can cream of chicken soup**
1	**can cream of mushroom soup**
1	**cup rice, cooked**

Brown 1st 2 ingredients together. **Drain**.
Add rest of ingredients.
Put in pam-sprayed 9x13 baking dish.
Bake at 350 degrees for 1 hour.

Vegetable Rice
"It's About Thyme"

1	(15 ounce) can kidney beans
1	(14.5 ounce) can stewed tomatoes
1	(10 ounce) bag frozen mixed vegetables
1	cup water
3/4	cup quick-cooking brown rice, uncooked
1/2	teaspoon thyme, crushed
2	dashes hot sauce
1	can tomato soup
1	(8 ounce) shredded Monterey Jack cheese

Combine 1st 7 ingredients in large saucepan.
Bring to a boil. **Reduce** Heat. **Cover**.
Simmer for 15 minutes or until rice is tender.
Stir in last 2 ingredients until heated thoroughly.

Q: Did you hear about the blonde coyote?
A: She got stuck in a trap, chewed off three of her legs and was still stuck.

Japanese Taco Rice
"Mexican Chel Bell"

1	pound ground beef, browned, drained
1	Tablespoon soy sauce
	Salt and pepper to taste
1	teaspoon garlic salt
2	cups rice, cooked
1	(8 ounce) shredded cheddar cheese
1	tomato, diced
1	(8 ounce) sour cream
1	(8 ounce) jar thick & chunky salsa

Combine 1st 4 ingredients together.
Add rice to meat mixture. **Mix** well.
Pour meat mixture into pam-sprayed baking dish.
Layer rest of ingredients in order given over mixture.
Refrigerate.

Georgie, Boy!

Barbara, a **blonde** in her fourth year as a freshman, sat in her US government class.

The professor asked Barbara if she knew what Roe vs. Wade was about.

Barbara pondered the question then finally said, "That was the decision George Washington had to make before he crossed the Delaware."

Chicken & Rice Vermicelli
"Dusty Chick With Brick"

1	box Rice-A-Roni chicken rice & vermicelli mix, cooked according to directions.
1	can cream of chicken soup
1/2	(14.5 ounce) can chicken broth
1/2	teaspoon salt
2	(4 ounce) cans chopped green chilies
2	chicken breasts, cooked, chopped
1	(8 ounce) sour cream
1	(8 ounce) shredded cheddar cheese
1	(2.8 ounce) can crispy fried onions

Mix 1st 7 ingredients together
Pour into pam-sprayed 9x13 baking dish.
Sprinkle cheese on top.
Bake at 350 degrees for 30-40 minutes.
Sprinkle onions on top. **Bake** 5 more minutes.

Q: Why can't blondes dial 911?
A: They can't find the 11 on the phone!

Ham & Rice Packets
"Wrapped For Reynolds"

3	cups rice, cooked
1	stick margarine, melted
1	cup cooked ham, diced
1	(8 ounce) can crushed pineapple
1/2	bell pepper, finely chopped
1/2	cup barbecue sauce

Combine all ingredients together.
Place individual servings of mixture on squares of foil, **bring** corners together and **twist**.
Bake at 350 degrees for 20 minutes.

Caramel Rice Pudding
"Russ Burn Her Debt"

3	cups rice, cooked
2	teaspoons vanilla
1	(14 ounce) can condensed milk
1	(12 ounce) can evaporated milk
1	Tablespoon sugar
1	teaspoon cinnamon

Mix all ingredients together.
Pour in pam-sprayed 9x13 baking dish.
Bake at 325 degrees for 1 hour.

South of the Border
(Mexican)

South of the Border
(Mexican)

Blondes In Mexico

Three women went down to Mexico one night to celebrate college graduation. They got drunk and woke up in jail, only to find that they were to be executed that morning. None of them could remember what they did the night before. The first one, a redhead, is strapped in the electric chair, and is asked if she has any last words. She says, "I just graduated from SMU and believe in the almighty power of God to intervene on behalf of the innocent." They throw the switch and nothing happens. They all immediately beg for her forgiveness and release her. The second one, a brunette, is strapped in and gives her last words, "I just graduated from Ole Miss Law School and I believe in the power of justice to intervene on the part of the innocent." They throw the switch and again, nothing happens. Again, they all immediately beg for her forgiveness and release her. The last one, a **blonde**, is strapped in and says, "Well, I'm from the University of Alabama and just graduated with a degree in Electrical Engineering, and I'll tell you right now, you ain't gonna electrocute nobody if you don't plug the plug in."

South Of The Border
(Mexican)

Green Chilies & Cheese Squares
"Blondzillas"

3 (4 ounce) cans chopped green chilies
1 (8 ounce) shredded Monterey Jack cheese
1 (8 ounce) shredded cheddar cheese
4 eggs, beaten
1 (12 ounce) can evaporated milk
   Salt to taste

Layer 1st 3 ingredients in pam-sprayed 8x8 baking dish.
Mix next 3 ingredients together.
Pour over top of cheese layers.
Bake at 350 degrees for 1 hour.
Cut into squares.

Fiesta Chicken Soup
"KiKi's Funky & Chunky"

1 (16 ounce) can refried beans
1 (14.5 ounce) can chicken broth
1 (15 ounce) can black beans
1 (15 ounce) can whole kernel corn, with liquid
1 (12 ounce) can chicken with liquid
1 cup chunky salsa

Combine all ingredients together.
Bring to a boil. **Reduce** heat. **Simmer** for 30 minutes.

South Of The Border
(Mexican)

Mexican Pasta Salad
"A Blonde Mexican Noodled"

1   (16 ounce) fettuccine, cooked according to package
1   Tablespoon olive oil
2   chicken breasts, cooked, diced
1   bell pepper, chopped
1   (16 ounce) shredded mozzarella cheese
1   red onion, diced
1   (16 ounce) bottle Italian salad dressing
1   teaspoon cumin
1   avocado, peeled, diced

Mix all ingredients together.

Mexi-Rice
"Dicey, Spicy, Ricey"

1   pound ground beef
1/2   onion, chopped
2   cups cooked rice
1   (8 ounce) can tomato sauce
1   can fiesta cheddar soup
1   package dry taco seasoning mix

Brown 1st 2 ingredients in large skillet. **Drain**.
Add next 4 ingredients to meat mixture.
Simmer for 5-10 minutes.

Crock-Pot Chilie Rellenos
"A Crock Of Spicy Redheads"

1   (4 ounce) can whole green chilies
1   (8 ounce) shredded Monterey Jack cheese
1   (8 ounce) shredded cheddar cheese
2   Tablespoons flour
2   eggs, beaten
1   (12 ounce) can evaporated milk
1   (8 ounce) can tomato sauce
     Salt to taste
     Pepper to taste

Spray crock-pot with pam.
Layer 1/2 chilies, 1/2 cheeses.
Combine last 6 ingredients.
Layer milk mixture over cheeses. **Repeat** layer.
Cover. **Cook** on low for 6-8 hours.

Q. Why was the blonde in the tree?
A. Because she was raking up the leaves!

South Of The Border
(Mexican)

Mexican Casserole
"On Day Lay, On Day Lay, Areva Areva"

2	pounds ground beef
1	onion, finely chopped
1	(14.5 ounce) can stewed tomatoes
2	(15 ounce) cans Mexican-style chili beans
1	cup rice, uncooked
1	(4 ounce) can chopped green chilies
1	package chili seasoning
	Salt & pepper to taste
1	(8 ounce) shredded cheddar cheese

Brown 1st 2 ingredients in large skillet. **Drain**.
Add next 6 ingredients. **Stir** thoroughly.
Simmer 20-25 minutes. **Add** cheese.
Simmer 5 more minutes.

Mexican Shrimp Cocktail
"Cock Tails Fiestaed"

1	cup Italian dressing
1	tomato, chopped
1	(4 ounce) can chopped green chilies
2	green onions, chopped
2	teaspoons hot pepper sauce
1	pound shrimp, cooked, peeled

Combine all ingredients together. **Cover**.
Marinate in refrigerator. **Stir** occasionally.

Pork Chops Olé
"A Waring Belynda"

6	**pork chops, center cut**
2	**Tablespoons oil**
	Salt to taste
1¹/₂	**cups water**
1	**(8 ounce) tomato sauce**
1	**package dry taco seasoning**
³/₄	**cup rice, uncooked, not instant**
1	**bell pepper, chopped**
1	**(8 ounce) shredded cheddar cheese**

Brown 1st 3 ingredients together. **Drain**.
Combine next 4 ingredients together.
Place rice in pam-sprayed 9x13 baking dish.
Place pork chops over rice. **Top** with peppers.
Cover. **Bake** at 350 degrees for 1¹/₂ hours.
Uncover. **Sprinkle** with cheese.
Return to oven until cheese melts.

Q: How does a blonde high-5?
A: She smacks herself in the forehead.

Salsa Chicken
"The Jern Again Salsa"

1	package dry taco seasoning mix
4	chicken breasts, boneless, skinless, cut in strips
2	Tablespoons oil
1	(14.5 ounce) can diced tomatoes
$^1/_3$	cup peach preserves
	Salt & pepper to taste

Combine 1st 2 ingredients in plastic bag. **Toss** to coat.
Place chicken in large skillet on medium heat.
Sauté for 5-10 minutes.
Stir in last 3 ingredients. **Cover**.
Simmer for 15 minutes.

Q: Why do blondes leave empty milk cartons in the fridge?
A: In case someone wants black coffee.

South Of The Border
(Mexican)

Margarita Cake
"Pearl De Mayo"

1 box yellow cake mix
1/2 stick margarine, softened
3 eggs, beaten
1/2 cup Blondarita mix
1/4 cup tequila (for a sober pearl, use water)
1/4 cup orange juice

Combine all ingredients together.
Pour in pam-sprayed bundt pan.
Bake at 325 degrees for 50-55 minutes.

Margarita Pie
"One Moore Shot"

1 1/2 cups pretzels, crushed,
1/2 cup sugar
1 stick margarine, melted
1 (21 ounce) can strawberry pie filling
1 (10 ounce) can frozen margarita mix, thawed
1 (8 ounce) frozen whipped topping, thawed

Combine pretzels with next 2 ingredients.
Press into pam-sprayed 9 inch pie plate.
Combine next 3 ingredients.
Spoon onto crust.
Freeze until firm.

Mexican Wedding Cake
"Here Comes The Jumping Bean"

2	cups sugar
2	eggs, beaten
2	cups self-rising flour
1	(20 ounce) can crushed pineapple
1	teaspoon vanilla

Combine all ingredients together.
Pour into pam-sprayed 9x13 baking dish.
Bake at 350 degrees for 1 hour.
Punch holes in cake while warm.

Topping:

1	(14 ounce) can sweetened condensed milk
1	can cream of coconut
1	(8 ounce) frozen whipped topping, thawed
$^1/_2$	cup coconut

Combine 1st 2 topping ingredients together.
Pour over warm cake.
Top with last 2 ingredients when cake is cool.

Q: Why can't blondes put in light bulbs?
A: They keep breaking them with their hammers.

Tailgating

Tailgating

Tailgating Blonde

A **blonde** was riding in the back of a pick-up truck when the truck went off the road and went into a pond. Some neighbors came out to see what happened and waited for the **blonde** to come out of the water. When she finally did, the neighbors asked her what took her so long. She replied, "I couldn't get the tailgate unlocked."

Ball
"He's All Balls"

1	(8 ounce) cream cheese, softened
1	(8 ounce) shredded sharp cheddar cheese
1	(8 ounce) shredded colby cheese
$1/2$	bell pepper, finely chopped
1	(2 ounce) jar chopped pimientos
2	teaspoons Worcestershire
$1/2$	teaspoon soy sauce
$1/2$	teaspoon hot sauce
	Dash of salt

Mix all ingredients together.
Form into 2 balls.
Serve with crackers

Bloody Mary Dip
"Mother Mary Is My Hero"

2	(8 ounce) cream cheese, softened
$1/2$	cup V-8 juice
$1/3$	cup tomato purée
1	bell pepper, finely chopped
2	ribs of celery, finely chopped
$1/3$	cup mayonnaise
	Horseradish to taste
	Lemon juice to taste
	Hot sauce to taste

Mix all ingredients together.
Serve with vegetables or crackers.

Cheese Bites
"Shapely Balls That Bite"

1	**(16 ounce) shredded sharp cheddar cheese**
1	**stick margarine, softened**
1	**cup self-rising flour**
1¹/₂	**cups cornflakes, crushed**
	Pinch of salt
	Cayenne pepper to taste

Cream 1ˢᵗ 2 ingredients together.
Add next 4 ingredients together. **Mix** well.
Roll into 1-inch balls.
Place on pam-sprayed cookie sheet.
Mash flat with a fork.
Bake at 350 degrees for 8-12 minutes.

Dill Bites
"Silly Jilly Bite"

1	**(6 ounce) box Chex rice cereal**
1	**stick margarine, melted**
¹/₂	**teaspoon salt**
¹/₄	**teaspoon pepper**
2	**teaspoons dill weed**
¹/₃	**cup parmesan cheese**

Pour cereal into large bowl.
Mix next 5 ingredients together.
Pour over cereal. **Mix** well.
Store in air-tight container.

Pepper Jelly Cheese Bites
"A Dye Her Bite"

1   **(8 ounce) shredded sharp cheddar cheese**
2   **sticks margarine, softened**
2   **cups all-purpose flour**
1   **teaspoon hot sauce**
1   **(10 ounce) jar Blonde Pepper Jelly**
2   **cups Rice Krispies**

Cream 1st 2 ingredients together. **Add** flour.
Add hot sauce and 1/2 cup of jelly.
Stir in Rice Krispies.
Shape into 1-inch balls.
Make a dent in each ball with thumb.
Fill with pepper jelly.
Bake at 350 degrees on ungreased cookie sheet for 8-12 minutes.

Corn Salsa
"Corny Blonde"

2   **(15 ounce) cans whole-kernel corn**
1   **(4 ounce) can chopped green chilies**
1   **(4 ounce) can chopped black olives**
1   **(4 ounce) can chopped jalapeños**
4   **Tablespoons balsamic vinegar**
1   **Tablespoon cajun seasoning**

Mix all ingredients together.
Serve with tortilla chips.

Black Bean Salsa
"Chi-O Chi-O It's Off To State We Go"

1   (14.5 ounce) can diced tomatoes
2   (14.5 ounce) cans black beans
1   (4 ounce) can chopped green chilies
1   (14 ounce) jar medium chunky salsa
1   teaspoon dried cilantro
1/8   teaspoon salt

Mix all ingredients together.
Serve with tortilla chips.

Crusty Stuffed Bites
"Come On Drum On"

1   package dry ranch dressing mix
1   (8 ounce) cream cheese, softened
1   (8 ounce) shredded mozzarella cheese
1   Tablespoon parmesan cheese
2   Tablespoons milk
2   (10 ounce) packages refrigerated pizza
    crust

Combine 1st 5 ingredients. **Set** aside.
Unroll pizza crust. **Spread** filling on crust.
Start at the longest end then roll up.
Slice each roll into 16 pieces.
Bake at 425 degrees on pam-sprayed cookie sheet for 8-12 minutes.

Football Party Dip
"Branning's Game Face"

4	(8 ounce) cream cheese, softened
2	packages dry ranch party dip
1	bell pepper, finely chopped
1	(4 ounce) can chopped black olives
2	(4 ounce) cans chopped green chilies
2	slices American cheese
1	(15 ounce) can whole black olives, drained
1/2	red pepper, cut into thin strips
	Crackers

Blend 1st 5 ingredients together. **Chill** 1 hour.
Using a spatula, **form** a football shape on a platter.
Chill 4 hours or overnight.
Decorate football with cheese slices, black olives, pepper strips.
Serve with crackers.

Q: What is every blonde's ambition?
A: To be like Vanna White and learn the alphabet.

Tailgating

Half-Time Salad
"Picasso's Halved"

1	**(16 ounce) can kidney beans**
1	**(12 ounce) can shoe peg corn**
1	**(15 ounce) can whole-kernel corn**
1	**(14.5 ounce) can French-style green beans**
1	**(15 ounce) can green peas**
1/2	**cup cider vinegar**
1/2	**cup sugar**
1/2	**cup olive oil**
3	**ribs of celery, finely chopped**

Drain liquid from 1st 5 ingredients.
Heat next 2 ingredients separately.
Remove from heat. **Add** last 2 ingredients.
Combine all ingredients together in large bowl.

Walking Tacos
"Walking to El Paso With Park"

2	**pounds ground beef, browned, drained**
2	**packets taco seasoning mix**
1	**can tomato soup**
1	**head lettuce, shredded**
2	**tomatoes, diced**
1	**(16 ounce) shredded cheddar cheese**
1	**(16 ounce) sour cream**
1	**(8 ounce) bottle taco sauce**
10	**single serving bags of corn chips**

Combine 1st 2 ingredients together according to seasoning directions.

Stir in tomato soup. **Heat** well.

Place in a wide-mouth thermos.

Put lettuce and tomatoes each in plastic containers.

When ready to eat **open** chip bag.

Squeeze bag to crush chips.

Place meat and toppings on crushed chips in bag.

Sprinkle with desired amount of taco sauce.

Eat with a plastic fork (unless you are at Ole Miss).

Q: Why do blondes shower for hours?
A: The shampoo bottle says, "Lather, rinse, and repeat!".

Hot Drummettes
"Spicy Drummond"

24	chicken drummettes
1	cup buttermilk
1	cup flour
$1/2$	teaspoon Blonde Lemon-Pepper
$1/2$	cup oil
2	cups Louisiana hot sauce
$1/2$	stick margarine
$1/2$	teaspoon salt & pepper, each
1	Tablespoon balsamic vinegar

Soak drummettes in buttermilk.
Roll drummettes in next 2 ingredients.
Fry in hot oil for 4-5 minutes.
Drain drummettes on paper towel.
Mix last 4 ingredients together.
Soak wings in sauce for 10 minutes.
Place into air tight container.

They All Look Alike!

Two **blondes** are walking down the street. One notices a compact on the sidewalk and leans down to pick it up. She opens it, looks in the mirror, and says, "Hmm this person looks familiar." The second **blonde** says, "Here, let me see!" So the first **blonde** hands her the compact. The second one looks in the mirror and says, "You dummy, it's me!"

Undercover

(Crockpot)

Undercover
(Crockpot)

Right Out From Under Me!

A **blonde** woman was driving a Porsche. She saw another **blonde** woman with a Porsche that had stopped on the side of the road. She stopped to ask what's wrong. The owner of the broken Porsche said, "I just looked under the hood, somebody stole my engine." The other **blonde** said, "Oh, don't worry, I have a spare one in the back of my car."

Black Eye Pea Dip
"I Relish A Tradition"

1 (8 ounce) Velvetta cheese, cubed
1 (15.5 ounce) can black-eyed peas
1 (4.5 ounce) can chopped green chilies
1 stick margarine
4 green onions, chopped
Tortilla chips

Combine 1st 5 ingredients in crock-pot.
Cover. **Cook** on low **stirring** until cheese melts.
Cook on low for 1-2 hours.
Serve with Tortilla chips.

Santa Fé Chicken Soup
"Do You Know The Way To Santa Fé?"

4 chicken breasts, chopped into 1 inch pieces
1 onion, finely chopped
1 (15 ounce) can whole-kernel corn, undrained
1 (24 ounce) can pinto beans, undrained
1 (14.5 ounce) can diced tomatoes, undrained
1 can diced rotel tomatoes
1 pound Velvetta cheese, cubed
1/4 cup milk
Salt & pepper to taste

Combine all ingredients together in crock-pot.
Cover. **Cook** on low 3-4 hours. **Do not** let soup boil.

Undercover
(Crockpot)

French Onion Soup
"No French Kiss For You"

1/2	stick margarine
3	Tablespoons olive oil
4	onions, thinly sliced
1	Tablespoon sugar
2	Tablespoons flour
2	cans beef broth
2	cans beef consommé
1/2	cup dry white wine
3	beef broth cans of water

Sauté 1st 3 ingredients together in large skillet.
Add next 2 ingredients. **Sauté** 2-3 more minutes.
Pour remaining ingredients & onion mixture in crock-pot.
Cover. **Cook** on low for 6-7 hours.

Doctor's Orders

A **blonde** is terribly overweight, so her doctor put her on a diet. "I want you to eat regularly for 2 days, then skip a day, and repeat this procedure for 2 weeks. The next time I see you, you'll have lost at least 5 pounds."

When the **blonde** returned, she shocked the doctor by losing nearly 20 pounds.

"Why, that's amazing!" the doctor said, "Did you follow my instructions?"

The **blonde** nodded, "I'll tell you though, I thought I was going to drop dead that 3rd day."

"From hunger, you mean?" asked the doctor.

"No, from all that skipping."

Stuffed Peppers
"Stuffed Instead Of Silicone"

6	bell peppers, cut off tops, clean seeds out
1	pound ground beef
1/2	onion, finely chopped
1	teaspoon salt
1	teaspoon pepper
1	cup rice, cooked
1	Tablespoon Worcestershire
1	(8 ounce) tomato sauce
1/4	cup beef broth

Boil peppers for 5 minutes in water. **Set** aside.
Brown next 2 ingredients in skillet. **Drain**.
Add next 4 ingredients. **Mix** well.
Stuff peppers with meat mixture.
Stand stuffed peppers upright in crock-pot.
Mix together last 2 ingredients. **Pour** over peppers.
Cover. **Cook** on low 5-7 hours.

Q: What is a cool refreshing drink for a blonde?
A: Perri-air.

Undercover
(Crockpot)

Creole Zucchini
"Abdalla Cabella"

6	zucchini, cut into $1/4$ inch slices
1	bell pepper, chopped
1	onion, chopped
1	teaspoon minced garlic
$1/2$	teaspoon salt
$1/4$	teaspoon pepper
1	(28 ounce) can diced tomatoes
2	Tablespoons margarine
2	Tablespoons parsley

Combine all ingredients in crock-pot.
Cover. **Cook** on high for 2 hours.

Italian Beef
"Rumped Italian"

3	pound rump roast
1	(8 ounce) can tomato sauce
$2^1/2$	cups water
1	teaspoon parsley
1	teaspoon garlic powder
1	teaspoon basil
1	teaspoon oregano
	Dash Worcestershire sauce
1	package dry Italian dressing mix

Place roast in crock-pot.
Combine remaining ingredients in saucepan.
Cook until boiling. **Pour** over roast in crock-pot.
Cook on low for 6-8 hours
Flake roast 1 hour before serving.

Chicken Cacciatore
"She's A Chicken And A Blonde Whiner"

1	(8 ounce) sliced fresh mushrooms
4	chicken breasts, boneless, skinless
1	(28 ounce) can diced tomatoes
1	package dry onion soup mix
$1/4$	cup red wine
$1/2$	teaspoon basil

Place mushrooms in crock-pot. **Add** chicken.
Combine remaining ingredients together.
Pour over chicken and mushrooms.
Cover. **Cook** on low for 8 hours.

Pineapple Chicken
" Hospitable Chick"

4	chicken breasts, boneless, skinless
1	(20 ounce) can pineapple tidbits, drained
2	Tablespoons Dijon mustard
	Dash of Soy sauce
1	teaspoon minced garlic
	Salt & pepper to taste

Place chicken in crock-pot.
Combine last 5 ingredients. **Pour** over chicken.
Cover. **Cook** on low for 7-9 hours.

Pork Chop Casserole
"Choppin' For Pork"

4	pork chops, center cut
2	Tablespoons oil
1	onion, sliced
1	can cream of mushroom soup
6	potatoes, peeled, sliced
8	slices American cheese

Brown 1st 2 ingredients in skillet.
Cover with onion slices.
Put 1st 3 ingredients in crockpot.
Layer last 3 ingredients on top of pork chops.
Cover. **Cook** on low for 6-8 hours.

Q: What is the definition of gross ignorance?
A: 144 blondes.

Orange Pork Roast
"He's A Juicy Porker"

1	onion, chopped
3	pound pork shoulder roast
1	(6 ounce) can frozen orange juice, thawed
$1/4$	cup brown sugar
$1/8$	teaspoon ground nutmeg
$1/2$	teaspoon each salt & pepper

Place onions in bottom of crock-pot.
Place roast over onions.
Mix next 5 ingredients together. **Pour** over roast.
Cover. **Cook** on high for 3 hours.
Reduce heat to low cook another 3 hours.
Remove roast and onions from crock-pot.
Cover. **Set** in oven on low to keep warm.
Skim fat from juices in crock-pot. **Pour** into large pan.

Gravy:

2	Tablespoons flour
2	Tablespoons water

Blend gravy ingredients in saucepan.
Bring to a boil, **stirring** frequently.
Serve gravy with roast and onions.

Crock Pot Candy
"No Need To Peek"

1   **(16 ounce) jar dry roasted peanuts, salted**
1   **(16 ounce) jar dry roasted peanuts, unsalted**
1   **(12 ounce) bag chocolate chips**
1   **(4 ounce) bar German chocolate, cut into pieces**
1   **(12 ounce) bag white chocolate chips**
1   **teaspoon vanilla**

Place all ingredients in crock-pot in order given.
Cover. **Cook** on low for 3 hours.
DO NOT REMOVE LID.
Turn off and let **cool** slightly.
Mix thoroughly. **Drop** by teaspoons onto wax paper.

Strawberry Delight
"Redheaded Afternoon Delight"

1   **(21 ounce) can strawberry pie filling**
1   **box strawberry cake mix**
1   **stick margarine, melted**
1   **teaspoon vanilla**
1/3   **cup pecans, chopped**
    Frozen whipped topping, thawed

Place pie filling in crock-pot.
Combine next 3 ingredients. **Sprinkle** over filling.
Sprinkle with pecans.
Cover. **Cook** on low for 2-3 hours.
Spoon whipped topping on dessert **when** ready to serve.

With Vegetables

With Vegetables

That Makes Sense

A **blonde** is driving down the road and sees a hitchhiker and offers him a ride. While driving along, the **blonde** sees the light about to turn red and hits the accelerator and speeds past the red light. Scared by this, the hitchhiker asks the **blonde** why she doesn't stop for the red light. The **blonde** said, "You see my older brother never stops for red lights and he's never had an accident."

While driving on, the **blonde** comes to another intersection and as soon as the light turned green she slammed on the brakes. "What are you doing?" said the hitchhiker "The light was green, why did you stop?" "Because," answered the **blonde** "My brother might be coming down the road, and I just told you, he doesn't stop for red lights."

Artichoke Bake
"Swallowin' and Chokin'

2	**(6 ounce) jars marinated artichoke hearts, chopped**
4	**eggs, beaten**
$^1/_4$	**cup Italian bread crumbs**
$^1/_8$	**teaspoon oregano**
$^1/_8$	**teaspoon hot sauce**
1	**(16 ounce) shredded cheddar cheese**

Mix all ingredients together.
Pour into pam-sprayed 9x9 baking dish.
Bake at 325 degrees for 30 minutes.

Broccoli Cheese Casserole
"Is He Bushy & Cheesy?"

1	**(10 ounce) bag chopped frozen broccoli**
1	**(16 ounce) carton small-curd cottage cheese**
1	**(8 ounce) shredded cheddar cheese**
4	**Tablespoons flour**
$^1/_2$	**stick margarine, melted**
4	**eggs, beaten**

Mix all ingredients together.
Pour into pam-sprayed 9x13 baking dish.
Bake at 350 degrees for 1 hour.

Asparagus & Swiss Cheese Casserole
"Oh Spare Us Kale!"

1/2	stick margarine
1	rib of celery, chopped
3	Tablespoons self-rising flour
1 1/2	cups milk
1	can cream of mushroom soup
1/2	pound Swiss cheese, cubed
2	eggs, hard-boiled, chopped
2	(12 ounce) cans asparagus
1	cup bread crumbs

Sauté 1st 2 ingredients in saucepan.
Add next 2 ingredients. **Cook**. **Stir** until thick.
Add next 3 ingredients to mixture.
Line asparagus in pam-sprayed 9x13 baking dish.
Pour sauce mixture over asparagus.
Top with bread crumbs.
Bake at 400 degrees for 20-30 minutes.

Q: Why couldn't the blonde write the number ELEVEN?
A: She didn't know which ONE came first.

French-Style Barbequed Beans
"A Qued French Kiss"

4	bacon slices, uncooked, cut in 2 inch pieces
$^1/_4$	cup onion, chopped
$^1/_2$	cup ketchup
1	Tablespoon Worcestershire
$^1/_4$	cup brown sugar
2	(14.5 ounce) cans French-style green beans, drained

Sauté 1st 2 ingredients in skillet until bacon is crispy.
Drain grease.
Add next 3 ingredients. **Simmer** for 5 minutes.
Place beans in pam-sprayed 9x13 baking dish.
Pour mixture over beans. Do **not stir**.
Bake at 350 degrees for 20 minutes.

Lost and Not Found!

One day a man came home from work and found his **blonde** wife leaning over the kitchen sink crying. He said, "What's wrong, Honey?" She said between sniffles, "I ... I dropped the ice cubes on the floor, and then I rinsed them off in hot water, and now I can't find them."

Corn Jalapeño Casserole
"Mikey is Hot & Corny"

1	onion, chopped
1	bell pepper, chopped
3	ribs of celery, chopped
1	stick of margarine
1	(8 ounce) shredded cheddar cheese
2	(15 ounce) cans cream-style corn
1	Tablespoon sugar
$^1/_2$	(4 ounce) can diced jalapeños
1	cup rice, cooked

Sauté 1st 4 ingredients together.
Combine all ingredients together.
Pour into pam-sprayed 9x13 baking dish.
Bake at 350 degrees for 45-50 minutes.

Bus Ride

A **blonde** was sitting on a bus next to a women holding a baby and the women was crying her heart out. "What's the matter?" asked the **blonde**. The lady replied, "When the bus conductor was collecting the tickets he said to me that he had never seen such an ugly baby in all his life." "You can't let him get away with that," said the **blonde.** "You go over there right now and hit him, and don't you worry, I'll hold your monkey for you."

With Vegetables

Eggplant-Tomatoes Bake
"A Blonde Matilda"

1	onion, finely chopped
1	(8 ounce) sliced fresh mushrooms
1	bell pepper, chopped
$^1/_4$	cup oil
1	eggplant, chopped in 1 inch cubes
3	tomatoes, chopped
2	eggs, beaten
1	cup Parmesan cheese
1	(8 ounce) Mozzarella cheese

Sauté 1st 4 ingredients together in large saucepan.
Add next 2 ingredients. **Simmer** covered for 25 minutes.
Combine last 3 ingredients.
Spoon $^1/_2$ eggplant mixture in pam-sprayed 2$^1/_2$ quart casserole dish.
Layer with $^1/_2$ cheese mixture. **Repeat** layers.
Bake at 375 degrees for 25 minutes.

Q: Why do restaurants never hire blondes to work at the take out door?
A: Because they always ask, "Is that for here or to go?"

Potatoes Barbequed
"What A Choice, Dale Or Joyce?"

¹/₂	stick margarine
¹/₄	cup flour
2	cups milk
¹/₄	teaspoon pepper
8	green onions, chopped
1	(8 ounce) shredded cheddar cheese
3	potatoes, boiled, peeled, sliced
1	bell pepper, cut in rings
¹/₂	cup barbecue sauce

Mix 1st 6 ingredients together in large saucepan.
Stir until cheese melts.
Layer potatoes, then sauce in pam-sprayed 9x13 dish.
Top with bell peppers and barbeque sauce.
Bake at 350 degrees for 25-35 minutes.

Be Prepared

A young **blonde** executive was leaving the office one evening when she noticed the CEO standing in front of the shredder with a piece of paper in his hand. "Listen," said the CEO, "This is important, my assistant has left for the day. Can you make this thing work?" "Certainly," she replies, flattered that the CEO had asked her for help. She turned the machine on, inserted the paper, and pressed the START button. "Excellent!" replied the CEO, "I'll need two copies."

Squash Delight
"Anne You're Squashed!"

4 yellow squash, sliced
1 onion, chopped
$^1/_4$ stick margarine
1 cup mayonnaise
3 eggs, beaten
1 package buttermilk ranch dressing mix
1 cup bread crumbs
$^1/_2$ stick margarine, melted
1 (8 ounce) shredded sharp cheddar cheese

Sauté first 3 ingredients in skillet until tender.
Add next 3 ingredients.
Pour into pam-sprayed 8x8 baking dish.
Combine last 3 ingredients together.
Spread over squash.
Bake at 325 degrees for 30-40 minutes.

Know Where You Are???

A policeman pulled a **blonde** over after she'd been driving the wrong way on a one-way street.

Cop, "Do you know where you were going?"

Blonde, "No, but wherever it is, it must be bad 'cause all the people were leaving."

With Vegetables

Tomato Wedge Casserole
"Wedged Against Bama"

3 tomatoes, cut into wedges
1 (8 ounce) shredded cheddar cheese
1 cup bread crumbs
1 bell pepper, chopped
1/2 onion, chopped
1/2 stick margarine, melted

Combine all ingredients together.
Pour in pam-sprayed 9x13 baking dish.
Bake at 350 degrees for 35-45 minutes.

English Pea Salad
"Pegged For Sweet Pea"

1/2 cup mayonnaise
2 Tablespoons sweet pickle relish
2 Tablespoons onion, finely chopped
1 (16 ounce) can English peas, drained
1 (8 ounce) shredded cheddar cheese
1 egg, hard boiled, chopped

Combine all ingredients together in bowl.
Refrigerate for 1 hour.

Q: What is a blonde's favorite part of a gas station?
A: The Air Pump!

Vegetable Casserole
"Frenchy Or Lizardy?"

2   (14.5 ounce) cans French-style green beans, drained
2   (15.25 ounce) cans gold & white corn mixed, drained
1   can cream of celery soup
1   (8 ounce) sour cream
1   (8 ounce) shredded cheddar cheese
1   teaspoon salt
$1/4$ teaspoon pepper

Mix all ingredients together.
Pour in pam-sprayed 9x13 baking dish.
Bake at 350 degrees for 30 minutes.

Topping:
1   (2.8 ounce) can French fried onions
$1/2$ stick margarine, melted

Combine topping ingredients together.
Pour over casserole.
Return to oven. **Broil** until onions are brown.

Q: Why did the blonde have tire tread marks on her back?
A: From crawling across the street when the sign said, "DON'T WALK".

Vegetable Delight
"I Bean Blonde A Long Time"

2   (14.5 ounce) cans French-style green beans
2   (15.25 ounce) cans lima beans
1   (16 ounce) can English peas
1   cup mayonnaise
1/2 onion, finely chopped
1   Tablespoon Worcestershire
2   Tablespoons margarine, melted
   Salt & pepper to taste
4   eggs, hard boiled, finely chopped

Heat 1st 3 ingredients for 10 minutes.
Pour off liquid. **Pour** in pam-sprayed $2^1/_2$ quart baking dish.
Combine next 5 ingredients in separate bowl.
Pour sauce over vegetables.
Bake at 350 degrees for 15-20 minutes.
Top with eggs.

Watch Your Break!

A **blonde** and a brunette were walking along a road and the **blonde** falls down a man hole. The brunette shouted down, "Have you broken anything?" The **blonde** shouts back, "There's nothing down here to break."

In The Winter

(Soups)

In The Winter
(Soups)

A Blonde In A Blizzard!

It was snowing heavily and blowing to the point that visibility was almost zero, when Donna, a **blonde**, got off work late one night. She managed to make her way to her car but wondered how she was going to make it home. Donna sat in her car while it warmed up and thought about her situation.

She finally remembered her daddy's advice: If she got caught in a blizzard, she should wait for a snowplow to come by and then follow it. That way she would not get stuck in a snowdrift.

Sure enough, in a little while a snowplow went by and Donna started to follow it. As she followed the snowplow, she was feeling very good because she was not having any problem with the blizzard conditions.

After quite some time had passed, Donna was somewhat surprised when the snowplow stopped, the driver got out, came back to her car, and signaled for her to roll down her window. The snowplow driver wanted to know if she was alright, as she had been following him for a long time. She said that she was fine, and told him of her daddy's advice to follow a snowplow when caught in a blizzard.

The driver replied that it was okay with him and she could continue if she wanted—but he was done with the Wal-Mart parking lot and was going over to K-Mart next.

8 Can Soup
"Can't You Tell I'm Canned?"

1   **pound ground beef, cooked, drained**
1   **(15 ounce) can stewed tomatoes**
1   **can tomato soup**
1   **(15 ounce) can vegetable soup**
1   **can Rotel tomatoes**
1   **(15 ounce) can chili with beans**
1   **(15 ounce) can whole kernel corn**
1   **(14.5 ounce) can cut green beans**
1   **(15 ounce) can Veg-all**

Combine all ingredients together.
Bring to a boil, **reduce** heat.
Simmer for 30 minutes, **stirring** occasionally.

Bean Soup
"A North State Gastro Needed"

2   **(15 ounce) cans pinto beans with jalapeños**
2   **(16 ounce) cans navy beans**
2   **(11.5 ounce) cans beans with bacon soup**
$^1/_2$ **onion, chopped**
1   **bell pepper, chopped**
1   **cup water**

Combine all ingredients together in a pot.
Bring to a boil, **reduce** heat.
Simmer for 30 minutes, **stirring** occasionally.

Butternut Squash Soup
"Squashed Blonde Nut"

1	butternut squash, chopped
1	rib celery, chopped
1	carrot, chopped
1	apple, peeled, chopped
3	(14.5 ounce) cans chicken broth
1	(pint) half & half

Combine all ingredients together in a pot.
Bring to a boil, **reduce** heat.
Simmer for 1 hour, **stirring** occasionally.

Cheese Soup
"Chel's Cheesy"

1	(14.5 ounce) can chicken broth
1	can cream of chicken soup
2	ribs of celery, chopped
1/2	onion, chopped
1	pound Velvetta cheese, cut in pieces
1	cup milk

Combine all ingredients in saucepan.
Bring to a boil, **reduce** heat.
Simmer for 1 hour, **stirring** occasionally.

Dill Pickle Soup
"Pickle, Tickle, Dickle & Nichols"

4	(14.5 ounce) cans chicken broth
2	chicken bouillon cubes
2	carrots, grated
2	potatoes, peeled, diced
3	ribs of celery, chopped
5	large dill pickles, grated
$^1/_2$	cup milk
3	Tablespoons flour
$^1/_2$	cup sour cream

Combine 1st 5 ingredients in large pot.
Cook covered until potatoes are tender, 10 minutes.
Add pickles, continue **cooking** for 15 minutes.
Mix milk and flour together.
Add mixture to soup. **Bring** to a boil, **stirring**.
Add sour cream. **Stir** until smooth.

Q: What did the blonde do when her friend said that she saw a hot guy in the cafeteria?
A: She ran over there and poured a bucket of water over him.

Macaroni & Cheese Soup
"Yankee Cheesy Noodle"

1	**(8 ounce) bag elbow macaroni**
¹/₂	**stick margarine**
¹/₂	**onion, finely chopped**
4	**cups milk**
1	**(16 ounce) shredded cheddar cheese**
1	**chicken bouillon cube**
2	**Tablespoons corn starch**
2	**Tablespoons water**
1	**(8 ounce) can whole kernel corn, drained**

Cook macaroni according to package. **Set** aside.
Sauté next 2 ingredients until tender. **Set** aside.
Combine milk and cheese in large saucepan.
Cook over medium heat, **stirring** until cheese melts.
Stir in bouillon cube.
Combine cornstarch and water together until smooth.
Add to milk mixture. **Cook** until thickened.
Stir in macaroni, onion mixture and corn.
Cook over low heat, **stirring** constantly.

Q: Did you hear about the two blondes that were found frozen to death in their car at the drive-in movie theater?
A: They went to see "Closed for Winter".

In The Winter
(Soups)

Minestrone-Gumbo Soup
"Neppie's Strone Mine"

1   pound ground beef, cooked, drained
2   cans minestrone soup
2   cans Home Style tomato soup
2   cans chicken gumbo soup
1   can diced Rotel tomatoes
4   cans water

Combine all ingredients together.
Bring to a boil. **Reduce** heat.
Simmer for 30 minutes, **stirring** occasionally.

Rotel Potato Soup
"Rolando's Roteling"

4   cups water
6   potatoes, peeled, diced
1   can cream of celery soup
1   can diced Rotel tomatoes
1   pound Velveeta cheese, cubed
    Salt & pepper to taste

Cook potatoes in water for 10 minutes until tender.
Add rest of ingredients.
Stir until cheese is melted.
Simmer for 1 hour, **stirring** occasionally.

Sour Cream Potato Soup
"Creamin' For A Tyler Man"

3	cups water
6	potatoes, peeled, diced
2	ribs celery, chopped
1/2	onion, chopped
2	cups milk
2	chicken bouillon cubes
1/2	stick margarine
1	(8 ounce) sour cream
1	Tablespoon flour

Cook potatoes in water for 10 minutes until tender.
Add rest of ingredients.
Simmer for 1 hour, **stirring** occasionally.

Turnip Green Soup
"Turn Her Green"

5	cups water
6	potatoes, peeled, diced
2	(16 ounce) cans navy beans
2	(10 ounce) bags frozen turnip greens
1	cup cooked ham, chopped
	Tabasco to taste

Cook potatoes in water 10 minutes until tender.
Add rest of ingredients.
Simmer for 1 hour, **stirring** occasionally.

Sausage Stroganoff Soup
"Link Me To Your Brick"

1 (12 ounce) package brown/serve sausage links, cut in $^1/_2$ inch slices, browned
1 (5 ounce) scalloped potato mix
3 cups water
1 (14.5 ounce) can chicken broth
1 (4.5 ounce) jar sliced mushrooms, drained
1 cup half & half
1 (8 ounce) sour cream
2 Tablespoons Dijon mustard
  Salt & pepper to taste

Combine 1st 5 ingredients in large saucepan.
Bring to a boil. **Reduce** heat.
Simmer uncovered for 15 minutes.
Stir in last 4 ingredients. **Simmer**.

Q: Why can't blondes eat jello?
A: They can't figure out how to fit two cups of water into those little packets.

Zesty Salsa Soup
"Any Blonde Can Salsa"

$^1/_2$	**pound pork sausage, browned, drained**
1	**(24 ounce) jar thick and chunky salsa**
1	**(16 ounce) can refried beans**
1	**(15 ounce) can pinto beans, drained**
1	**can beef broth**
1	**(4 ounce) can chopped green chilies**

Combine all ingredients together in pot.
Bring to a boil. **Reduce** heat.
Simmer for 30 minutes, **stirring** occasionally.

Blonde Men's 2 x 4's!

A couple of **blonde** men in a pickup truck drove into a lumberyard. One of the **blonde** men walked in the office and said, "We need some four-by-twos." The clerk said, "You mean two-by-fours, don't you?" The man said, "I'll go check," and went back to the truck. He returned a minute later and said, "Yeah, I meant two-by-fours." "Alright. How long do you need them?" The **blonde** paused for a minute and said, "I'd better go check." After awhile, the **blonde** returned to the office and said, "A long time. We're gonna build a house."

X-Tra Grainy

(Breads)

X-Tra Grainy
(Breads)

Bowling Blondes

Two bowling teams, one made up of all **blondes** and one of all brunettes, charter a double-decker bus for a weekend tournament in Atlantic City. The brunette team rode in the bottom deck of the bus and the **blonde** team rode on the top level. The brunette team down below was whooping it up and having a great time when one of them realized she didn't hear anything from the **blondes** upstairs. She decided to go up and investigate. When the brunette reached the top, she found all the **blondes** frozen in fear, staring straight ahead at the road and clutching the seats in front of them. The brunette asked, "What is going on up here? We're having a great time downstairs!" One of the **blondes** said, "Yeah, but you've got a driver!"

Chocolate Bread
"Chocolate Over Sex"

1	**box chocolate cake mix**
1	**small box instant vanilla pudding**
1/4	**cup oil**
4	**eggs, beaten**
1	**cup hot water**
1	**teaspoon vanilla**

Mix all ingredients together.
Pour batter into 2 pam-sprayed loaf pans.
Bake at 350 degrees for 35-45 minutes.

Jalapeño Bread
"Hub Bored Membranes"

1/2	**onion, chopped**
1	**stick margarine**
1/2	**(4 ounce) can chopped jalapeño peppers**
1	**cup parmesan cheese**
1/4	**cup bacon bits**
2	**(10 count) biscuits, not flaky**

Sauté onion in margarine.
Add next 3 ingredients.
Cut biscuits into fourths.
Toss biscuit pieces in mixture.
Place into pam-sprayed bundt pan.
Bake at 325 degrees for 30-40 minutes.

Pistachio Nut Bread
"Antiquity's Nuts"

1	**box yellow cake mix**
1	**small box instant pistachio pudding**
1	**(8 ounce) sour cream**
$^1/_2$	**teaspoon almond extract**
4	**eggs, beaten**
$^1/_2$	**cup oil**

Mix all ingredients together.
Pour $^1/_2$ batter into 2 pam-sprayed loaf pans.

Topping:
$^1/_2$	**cup sugar**
1	**teaspoon cinnamon**
$^1/_2$	**cup pecans, finely chopped**

Mix all topping ingredients together.
Pour $^1/_2$ topping over batter in pans.
Pour remaining batter over topping.
Sprinkle with remaining topping.
Bake at 350 degrees for 50-60 minutes.

Q: Why did the blonde throw a puppy on a bun in the microwave?
A: She wanted a hotdog.

X-Tra Grainy
(Breads)

French Cheesy Bread
"No Frenchy Kissey"

1	loaf of French bread
$^1/_2$	cup mayonnaise
1	stick margarine, melted
1	(4 ounce) can chopped green chilies
1	(8 ounce) shredded Monterey Jack cheese
$^1/_2$	teaspoon garlic salt

Slice bread in half lengthwise.
Combine next 5 ingredients.
Spread on each side of bread.
Broil until bubbly.

Banana Split Muffins
"Barrel Full Of Monkeys"

$1^1/_2$	cups self-rising flour
1	cup sugar
1	(6 ounce) bag chocolate chips
$^1/_2$	cup pecans, chopped
3	ripe bananas, mashed
$^1/_2$	cup mayonnaise

Combine 1st 4 ingredients together.
Combine last 2 ingredients in separate bowl.
Combine all ingredients together.
Spoon into pam-sprayed muffin tins.
Bake at 375 degrees for 15-20 minutes.

Key Lime Muffins
"Tarty Smarty Billy Bob"

$^1/_2$	stick margarine, softened
$^1/_2$	cup sugar
2	eggs, beaten
$^1/_4$	cup lime juice
1$^1/_2$	teaspoons lime zest
1	(8 ounce) container key lime or plain yogurt
2	cups self-rising flour

Cream 1st 6 ingredients together.
Add flour to mixture. Batter will be stiff.
Spoon into pam-sprayed muffin tins.
Bake at 350 degrees for 15-20 minutes.

Glaze:

> **Juice of 1 lime**
> **Sugar**

Combine glaze ingredients together.
Dip top of hot muffins in glaze.

Q: What did the blonde do when she broke her Tupperware?
A: Called the plastic surgeon.

Oreo Muffins
"Double Stuffed Muffs"

1³/₄ cups self-rising flour
¹/₂ cup sugar
³/₄ cup milk
¹/₃ cup sour cream
1 egg, beaten
¹/₂ stick margarine, melted
1 teaspoon vanilla
¹/₂ teaspoon almond extract
20 Oreo cookies, coarsely crushed

Mix 1ˢᵗ 8 ingredients together in large bowl.
Stir in cookies gently.
Spoon batter into pam-sprayed muffin tins.
Bake at 400 degrees for 15-20 minutes.

Pumpkin Muffins
"Strawberry Blonde Muff"

2 cups sugar
1 cup oil
4 eggs, beaten
1 (16 ounce) can pumpkin
2 cups self-rising flour
1 teaspoon cinnamon

Mix all ingredients together.
Pour in pam-sprayed muffin tins.
Bake at 325 degrees for 20-25 minutes.

X-Tra Grainy
(Breads)

Blueberry Breakfast Rolls
"Rollin' In Blue Dough"

1   **(10 ounce) can refrigerated pizza crust dough**

Blueberry Filling:
- **³/₄**   **cup fresh or frozen blueberries**
- **2**   **Tablespoons orange juice**
- **2**   **Tablespoons sugar**
- **2**   **teaspoons cornstarch**
- **1**   **teaspoon grated orange peel**

Combine all filling ingredients together in saucepan.
Cook over medium heat until thick & bubbly.
Cook about 3 minutes. **Cool** for about 10 minutes.
Unroll pizza dough on lightly floured surface.
Pat into a 9x12 rectangle. **Spread** filling over dough.
Leave a ¹/₂ inch border along the sides.
Roll up dough and **seal** seams.
Cut roll into 12 one inch slices.
Place in pam-sprayed muffin tins.
Bake at 350 degrees for 12-15 minutes.

Glaze:
- **¹/₂**   **cup powdered sugar**
- **1**   **Tablespoon milk**
- **¹/₂**   **teaspoon grated orange peel**

Combine all glaze ingredients together.
Drizzle over rolls.

Butterscotch Cinnamon Rolls
"Bills Rollin' In Scotch"

2	**(8 ounce) cans refrigerated crescent rolls, separated**
1	**small box butterscotch pudding, not instant**
1	**stick margarine**
³/4	**cup brown sugar**
³/4	**Tablespoon cinnamon**
¹/2	**cup pecans, chopped**

Arrange rolls in pam-sprayed bundt pan.
Sprinkle dry pudding mix over rolls.
Cook last 4 ingredients until sugar is dissolved.
Make sure mixture bubbles. **Pour** over rolls.
Cover tightly with foil. **Let stand** overnight.
Bake at 350 degrees for 30 minutes.

Windows 2005

A **blonde**, called the Canon help desk with a problem with her printer. The tech asked her if she was running it under Windows. The woman responded, "No, my desk is next to the door. But that's a good point. The man sitting in the cubicle next to me is under a window, and his is working fine."

Maple Crescent Pull-Aparts
"Sticky Pulling Her Apart"

1/2	**stick margarine, melted**
1/4	**cup brown sugar**
2	**Tablespoons syrup**
1	**(8 ounce) can refrigerated crescent rolls**
4	**Tablespoons sugar**
1	**teaspoon cinnamon**

Combine 1st 3 ingredients together.
Pour in ungreased 9 inch cake pan.
Remove dough from can in 2 rolled sections.
Do not unroll dough. **Cut** each roll of dough into 6 slices.
Combine last 2 ingredients together.
Dip both sides of each slice in sugar mixture.
Arrange slices in cake pan.
Sprinkle with any remaining sugar mixture.
Bake at 375 degrees for 15-20 minutes.

The Blonde And The Post Office

A **blonde** goes to the post office to buy stamps for her Christmas cards.

She says to the clerk, "May I have 50 Christmas stamps?"
The clerk says, "What denomination?"

The woman says, "Has it come to this? Give me 6 Catholic, 12 Presbyterian, 10 Lutheran and 22 Baptists."

Marshmallow Rolls
"Sticky & Sugary"

1	**Tablespoon sugar**
$1/4$	**teaspoon cinnamon**
1	**Tablespoon margarine, melted**
8	**large marshmallows**
1	**(8 ounce) can refrigerated crescent rolls**
	Powdered sugar

Combine 1st 2 ingredients together.
Roll marshmallows in margarine, then cinnamon/sugar.
Wrap each marshmallow in a roll, completely covered.
Place wrapped marshmallow in pam-sprayed muffin tin.
Bake at 375 degrees for 10-12 minutes.
Remove immediately from muffin cups.
Sprinkle with powdered sugar.

Q: Why did the blonde have to drink a hot drink?
A: Because she couldn't fit any ice into the bottle.

X-Tra Grainy
(Breads)

No Match For A Blonde

A **blonde** and a lawyer are seated next to each other on a flight from Los Angeles to New York. The lawyer asks if she would like to play a fun game. The **blonde**, tired, just wants to take a nap, so she politely declines and rolls over to the window to catch a few winks. The lawyer persists and explains that the game is easy and a lot of fun. He says, "I ask you a question, and if you don't know the answer, you pay me $5, and vice versa." Again, she declines and tries to get some sleep. The lawyer, now agitated, says, "Okay, if you don't know the answer, you pay me $5, and if I don't know the answer, I will pay you $500." This catches the **blonde's** attention and figuring there will be no end to this torment, agrees to the game. The lawyer asks the first question, "What's the distance from the earth to the moon?" The **blonde** doesn't say a word, reaches into her purse, pulls out a $5.00 bill, and hands it to the lawyer. "Okay," says the lawyer, "Your turn." She asks, "What goes up a hill with three legs and comes down with four legs?" The lawyer, puzzled, takes out his laptop computer and searches all his references ... no answer. Frustrated, he sends e-mails to all his friends and co-workers but to no avail. After an hour, he wakes the **blonde** and hands her $500. The **blonde** thanks him and turns back to get some more sleep. The lawyer, who is more than a little miffed, stirs the **blonde** and asks, "Well, what's the answer?" Without a word, the **blonde** reaches into her purse, hands the lawyer $5, and goes back to sleep.

Cook?

A Fish Tale!

Three **blondes** were sitting by the side of a river holding fishing poles with the lines in the water. A game warden came up behind them, tapped one on the shoulder and said, "Excuse me ladies, I'd like to see your fishing licenses."

"We don't have any," replied the first blonde.

"Well, if you're going to fish, you need fishing licenses."

"But officer," replied the second **blonde**, "We aren't fishing. We all have magnets at the end of our lines and we're collecting debris off the bottom of the river."

The warden lifted up all the lines and, sure enough, there were magnets tied to the end of each line. "Well, I know of no law against it," said the warden, "Take all the debris you want." And with that, he left.

As soon as he was out of sight, the three **blondes** started laughing hysterically. "What a dumb cop," the second **blonde** said to the other two, "Doesn't he know that there are steelhead trout in this river?!"

Below Flood Stage

A milkman sees a note on the door of one of his **blonde** customers. The note asks for 100 quarts of milk. Thinking this was a mistake, the milkman rings her doorbell and asks about the 100 quarts. She says, "Yes, I need 100 quarts. On the talk show I saw last night they said milk baths are good for the skin." The milkman asks, "Do you want it PASTEURIZED?" She answers, "No...up to my shoulders will be sufficient!"

At The Zoo

(Kiddy Food)

At The Zoo
(Kiddy Food)

Mass Transit Blonde

A **blonde** is visiting Washington, DC. This is her first time to the city, so she wants to see the Capitol building. Unfortunately, she can't find it, so she asks a police officer for directions. "Excuse me, officer," the **blonde** says, "How do I get to the Capitol building?" The officer says, "Wait here at this bus stop for the number 54 bus. It'll take you right there." The **blonde** thanks the officer and he drives off. Three hours later the police officer comes back to the same area and the **blonde** is still waiting at the same bus stop. The officer gets out of his car and says, "Excuse me, but to get to the Capitol building, I said to wait here for the number 54 bus. That was three hours ago. Why are you still waiting?" The **blonde** says, "Don't worry, officer, it won't be long now. The 45th bus just went by."

Cheetah Footprints

1¹/₂	cups graham cracker crumbs
1	stick margarine, melted
1	teaspoon vanilla
1	(14 ounce) can sweetened condensed milk
1	(12 ounce) bag chocolate chips
1	(6 ounce) bag peanut butter chips

Place crumbs in pam-sprayed 9x13 baking dish.
Mix next 2 ingredients together. **Pour** over crumbs.
Pour condensed milk evenly over crumbs.
Top with chips, pressing down firmly.
Bake at 350 degrees for 20 minutes.
Cut into bars.

Dinosaur Dirt Cookies

¹/₄	cup cocoa (dirt)
¹/₂	cup water (swamp water)
2	cups sugar (crushed bones)
1	stick margarine (fat)
2	cups oatmeal (dried grass)
¹/₂	cup peanut butter (squashed bugs)

Mix 1st 4 ingredients together in saucepan.
Heat to boiling. **Add** oatmeal.
Remove from heat. **Add** peanut butter.
Mix. **Spoon** on wax paper.

Giraffe Goulash Pie

$2/3$	cup creamy peanut butter
1	small box instant chocolate pudding
2	cups milk
1	(8 ounce) frozen whipped topping, thawed
6	Oreos, crushed
1	(6 ounce) chocolate ready crust

Mix 1st 5 ingredients together.
Pour into pie crust.
Refrigerate.

Grizzly Bear Munch

1	(13 ounce) box honey graham cereal
1	(10 ounce) Teddy Honey graham cookies
1	package ramen noodles, crushed, no seasoning
$1/2$	cup sliced almonds
$1/3$	cup margarine
$1/3$	cup honey

Mix 1st 4 ingredients together in large bowl.
Mix last 2 ingredients in saucepan over low heat.
Pour over honey graham mixture. **Toss** to coat.
Spread mixture on large baking sheet.
Bake at 350 degrees for 10 minutes. **Stir** occasionally.

Q: What is the difference between Elvis and smart blondes?
A: Elvis has been sighted.

At The Zoo
(Kiddy Food)

Hippo Chow

1	**(15.6 ounce) Chex rice cereal**
1	**(6 ounce) bag chocolate chips**
$1/2$	**cup creamy peanut butter**
$1/2$	**stick margarine**
1	**teaspoon vanilla**
$1^1/2$	**cups powdered sugar**

Place cereal in a large bowl.
Melt next 4 ingredients in microwave until creamy.
Pour over cereal until evenly coated.
Put powdered sugar in a large plastic bag.
Add coated cereal. **Shake** until evenly coated.
Spread over a sheet of wax paper until cooled.
Store in refrigerator in airtight container.

Kangaroo Kookies

$2/3$	**cup sugar**
$2/3$	**cup Karo syrup**
$1^1/4$	**cup crunchy peanut butter**
1	**teaspoon vanilla**
3	**cups cornflakes**
	Powdered sugar

Bring 1st 2 ingredients to a boil in saucepan.
Add next 2 ingredients.
Stir until mixed. **Pour** in cornflakes.
Drop by spoonfuls on wax paper.
Sprinkle with powdered sugar.

Monkey Doing The Splits

1   **(14 ounce) can sweetened condensed milk**
1   **(12 ounce) frozen whipped topping, thawed**
1   **(21 ounce) can cherry pie filling**
3   **medium firm bananas, cut into chunks**
1   **(8 ounce) can crushed pineapple, drained**
¹/₂ **cup pecans, chopped**

Combine 1ˢᵗ 2 ingredients together.
Add next 4 ingredients to condensed milk mixture.
Pour into 9x13 dish. **Refrigerate**.

Polar Bear Brains

1   **(7 ounce) bag flaked coconut**
¹/₂ **stick margarine, softened**
¹/₄ **cup half & half**
1   **(16 ounce) box powdered sugar**
1   **teaspoon vanilla**
¹/₈ **teaspoon almond extract**

Mix all ingredients together in large bowl.
Line cookie sheet with wax paper.
Drop by spoonfuls on wax paper.
Refrigerate at least one hour.
Serve chilled.

Q: Why do blondes cross the street?
A: To catch the air.

Raccoons

1	**(20 ounce) bag Oreo cookies**
1/2	**stick margarine, softened**
1	**(8 ounce) cream cheese, softened**
1	**cup powdered sugar**
2	**small boxes French vanilla instant pudding**
3 1/2	**cups milk**

Crush Oreos in a blender.
Cream next 3 ingredients. **Set** aside.
Mix last 2 ingredients together.
Layer in 8x8 dish: Oreos, cream cheese mixture, pudding.
Refrigerate to set before serving.

Spider Web Pizza

1	**(20 ounce) chocolate chip cookie dough**
2	**(8 ounce) cream cheese, softened**
1/2	**cup sugar**
1/2	**teaspoon vanilla**
2	**eggs, beaten**
2	**squares semi-sweet baking chocolate, melted**

Press cookie dough on pam-sprayed pizza pan.
Cream next 4 ingredients together.
Spread on cookie dough.
Bake at 350 degrees for 20 minutes.
Drizzle with melted chocolate.

At The Zoo
(Kiddy Food)

Tigers Totally Terrizing

1	(12 ounce) Total whole grain cereal
3/4	cup brown sugar
1	(6 ounce) bag butterscotch chips
1	(6 ounce) bag chocolate chips
1	(6.25 ounce) can peanuts
1	stick margarine, melted

Combine 1st 5 ingredients together.
Drizzle with margarine. **Toss**.

Zebra Cupcakes

1	box chocolate cake mix
1	(8 ounce) cream cheese, softened
1/3	cup sugar
1	egg, beaten
	Dash of salt
1	(6 ounce) bag chocolate chips

Mix cake according to package directions.
Spoon cake batter into pam-sprayed muffin tins 2/3 full.
Cream next 4 ingredients together.
Stir in chocolate chips.
Drop a teaspoon of cheese mixture into each cupcake.
Bake at 350 degrees for 15 minutes.

Q: Why don't you give a blonde a coal truck to drive?
A: It takes her nine months to deliver it.

Index

Index

280

Index

Any Blonde Can Do It!

Please send _____ copy(ies)   @ $19.95 each_____

Postage and Handling   @ $ 5.00 each_____

Mississippi residents add 7% sales tax   @ $ 1.40 each_____

                                               TOTAL _____

Name _____

Address _____

City _____ State _____ Zip _____

Make checks payable to
Any Blonde Can Do It!
P. O. Box 320747
Flowood, MS 39232

Credit Cards accepted (check one)
_____ Visa   _____ MasterCard

Number:_____ Expiration: _____

Cardholder's signature: _____

Phone number:_____

Any Blonde Can Do It!

Please send _____ copy(ies)   @ $19.95 each_____

Postage and Handling   @ $ 5.00 each_____

Mississippi residents add 7% sales tax   @ $ 1.40 each_____

                                               TOTAL _____

Name _____

Address _____

City _____ State _____ Zip _____

Make checks payable to
Any Blonde Can Do It!
P. O. Box 320747
Flowood, MS 39232

Credit Cards accepted (check one)
_____ Visa   _____ MasterCard

Number:_____ Expiration: _____

Cardholder's signature: _____

Phone number:_____

Any Blonde Can Do It!

Please send _____ copy(ies)   @ $19.95 each_____

Postage and Handling   @ $ 5.00 each_____

Mississippi residents add 7% sales tax @ $ 1.40 each_____

                                        TOTAL _____

Name _____

Address _____

City _____ State _____ Zip _____

Make checks payable to
Any Blonde Can Do It!
P. O. Box 320747
Flowood, MS 39232

Credit Cards accepted (check one)
_____ Visa   _____ MasterCard

Number:_____ Expiration: _____

Cardholder's signature: _____

Phone number: _____

Any Blonde Can Do It!

Please send _____ copy(ies)   @ $19.95 each_____

Postage and Handling   @ $ 5.00 each_____

Mississippi residents add 7% sales tax @ $ 1.40 each_____

                                        TOTAL _____

Name _____

Address _____

City _____ State _____ Zip _____

Make checks payable to
Any Blonde Can Do It!
P. O. Box 320747
Flowood, MS 39232

Credit Cards accepted (check one)
_____ Visa   _____ MasterCard

Number:_____ Expiration: _____

Cardholder's signature: _____

Phone number: _____